T0339202

"Most of our churches need to teach their people more clearly what the mission of God in the world is all about, need to align their own missions more closely with God's mission, and need to do so from the Bible—unpacking God's purposes for us more fully than the usual passing references to the Great Commission do. This book by J. D. Payne will help them do these things. It offers a whole-Bible theology of mission that demonstrates that God is glorified in the blessing of the nations with the gospel. I pray that many read it and respond with greater resolve to play their part in God's drama of redemption."

**Douglas A. Sweeney**
dean, Beeson Divinity School

"Goldilocks found that some of the porridge was too hot, some too cold, and one bowl just right. Similarly, many books on the theology of mission can either be too superficial or too detailed (dense!). J. D. Payne has provided an invaluable service to his readers by writing a text that is 'just right'—just right in depth of biblical reflection, scholarly engagement, and practical application. This book is my number 1 recommended text for a biblical theology of mission."

**Robert L. Plummer**
Collin and Evelyn Aikman Professor of Biblical Studies,
The Southern Baptist Theological Seminary

"As a missional hermeneutic continues to take hold among biblical scholars and missiologists it is yielding rich fruit. J. D. Payne's *Theology of Mission* is a great example of this. Attentive to the unifying thread of mission and to the diversity of the missional context in different parts of the scriptural canon, Payne provides deepening insight into the rich kaleidoscope of mission in Scripture. Highly recommended for those who want to be growingly faithful to their missional identity."

**Michael W. Goheen**
professor of missional theology,
Covenant Theological Seminary

# THEOLOGY OF MISSION

*A Concise Biblical Theology*

# THEOLOGY OF MISSION

## A Concise Biblical Theology

J. D. PAYNE

LEXHAM PRESS

*Theology of Mission: A Concise Biblical Theology*

Copyright 2021 J. D. Payne

Lexham Press, 1313 Commercial St., Bellingham, WA 98225
LexhamPress.com

Print ISBN 9781683595724
Digital ISBN 9781683595755
Library of Congress Control Number 2021941978

Lexham Editorial: Todd Hains, Jake Raabe, Kelsey Matthews, Jessi Strong, Mandi Newell
Cover Design: Lydia Dahl, Brittany Schrock
Typesetting: Abigail Stocker

*To the One who was in the beginning and coming soon,*
*and to Sarah, his amazing blessing to me*

# Contents

# Preface

**W**HENEVER I ASK a class for biblical support of God's mission in the world, the Matthean account of the Great Commission (Matt 28:18–20) is usually the first passage referenced. Of course, there is nothing wrong with pointing to this Scripture. Whenever I ask for another passage, Acts 1:8 is often stated, then a general reference to Paul's missionary journeys. Beyond these, I usually receive no additional support.

Why is this the case? Is this all there is in the Bible when it comes to God's mission—just a few texts? God has chosen to reveal himself through many books, and is his mission only connected to a few sentences in two books? Is this all the Bible provides on the topic? Have we allowed a few verses to be the primary support system for the church's modern apostolic work? While Matthew 28:18–20 is a rich text and incredibly important to the church's task, there is so much more in the Bible related to God's mission. In fact, the global mission task would still be valid even if Jesus never spoke those words.[1]

Throughout the twentieth century, mission came to mean a variety of activities. Little has changed today. The church frequently engages in actions labeled "missions," even if the gospel of Jesus Christ is never shared! We continue to reside in a world of competing voices, some better than others. This is true within the church and outside the church. We need to know what is contained in the Scriptures, especially when it comes to such an important topic as our study. Theology shapes Christian decision-making.[2]

---

1. David J. Bosch, "Hermeneutical Principles in the Biblical Foundation for Mission," *Evangelical Review of Theology* 17 (1993): 439.

2. Andrew F. Walls, "Mission History as the Substructure of Mission Theology," *Swedish Missiological Themes* 93, no. 3 (2005): 374.

## MISSION, BLESSING THE
## NATIONS, AND SUB-THEMES

The purpose of this book is to trace the biblical theme of mission throughout the Scriptures by considering how God is glorified through the blessing of the nations. In the general sense, mission is all God is doing in the cosmos to accomplish his will. While there are many definitions of mission among scholars, I am using it here to refer to all that God has done, is doing, and will do to redeem sinful humans and recreate the cosmos into the new heaven and earth. God works through personal means in ways only assigned to divine prerogative to accomplish this purpose. However, his primary means toward this work, noted throughout the Scriptures, involves his people. This book addresses both.

Diversity and unity are found within the Old and New Testaments. Numerous themes bring the Scriptures together to tell a single story. There are many ways to approach the study of biblical theology of mission and trace a particular topic throughout the Bible.[3] Scholars have often noted the storyline of the Bible relates to the concepts of creation, fall, redemption, and restoration. From Genesis to Revelation, the reader is never far from any of these significant moments. With these in mind, this book attempts to address how God's mission is revealed in the story.[4] One way to understand this overarching theme is to consider several sub-themes that provide support derived from the biblical texts.[5] The primary method used in this book is an inductive exegesis that leads to a biblical theology. This biblical-theological approach is combined with a salvation-historical approach to examine various portions of the Scriptures related to mission.

---

3. For example David Baker argues that there are six key aspects to the relationship between the Old and New Testaments: 1) theological unity in Christ; 2) salvation-history; 3) typology; 4) promise and fulfillment; 5) continuity and discontinuity; and 6) covenant. See David Baker, *Two Testaments, One Bible: The Theological Relationship Between the Old and New Testaments,* 3rd ed. (Downers Grove, IL: IVP Academic, 2010), 271–76.

4. It should be noted that this book is written with the caution in mind about the problems of a single center to biblical theology. See Graeme Goldsworthy, *Christ-Centered Biblical Theology: Hermeneutical Foundations and Principles* (Downers Grove, IL: IVP Academic, 2012), 216.

5. As an example of understanding subthemes in major themes related to biblical theology, see Charles H. H. Scobie, *The Ways of Our God: An Approach to Biblical Theology* (Grand Rapids: Eerdmans, 2003), 93–99.

However, while the mission of God provides a unifying approach to understanding the biblical story, the Bible is filled with complexity. Each of the sub-themes addressed will not be found in every book. Though the mission of God recapitulates from Genesis to Revelation, some sub-themes will find greater representation than others. Given the diversity of the Scriptures, some will run extensively throughout the books, but others will be noted to a lesser degree. No text is totally irrelevant to God's purpose in the cosmos.[6] This approach provides a more robust understanding of the mission of God than an approach that only addresses a few of the significant sub-themes.

## PATTERN OF PURPOSE
## THROUGHOUT SCRIPTURE

The glory of God among his image-bearers comes through sending and relationship. It is in and through relationship that the nations are blessed with the expectation they will enjoy such benefits and leverage them for God's glory among others. There is a particular pattern that repeats itself throughout the Scriptures in relation to God's mission: sending to the world → proclaiming hope through judgment → entering relationship → receiving blessing. God takes the initiative and comes to his creation, or sends his representative(s). A message of hope is shared but reveals that his good news involves judgment and consequences for sin. Those who embrace God's message by faith enter into relationship with him and his kingdom people and experience his blessings.

From Genesis to Revelation, God's purpose and work in the world reveals a God who receives glory through relationship and blessing. At creation, he blesses man and woman (Gen 1:28); his promise to Abraham involves blessing (Gen 12:1–3); life in the kingdom involves blessing (Matt 5:1–11); and Revelation concludes with blessing to those able to enter the new Jerusalem (Rev 22:14). While relationship with God brings such favor, his benefits (Psalm 103:2) were not given simply for selfish consumption. Though to be enjoyed, the blessings were to be used appropriately to glorify

---

6. Graeme Goldsworthy, *Preaching the Whole Bible as Christian Scripture* (Grand Rapids: Eerdmans, 2000). For an example of this perspective see Tim J. Davy, *The Book of Job and the Mission of God: A Missional Reading* (Eugene, OR: Pickwick, 2020) where the author notes that Job stands apart from the general story of God's mission but speaks into it (128).

himself. The psalmist was quick to note the relationship between receiving the blessings of God and God's glory among the nations (Psalm 67). It was Israel's failure to follow such desire that resulted in the selfish transformation of her blessings into the idols that resulted in Assyrian and Babylonian captivity.

Prior to the fall, God comes to Adam and Eve, enters into relationship, and blesses them. As his image-bearers, they were to populate the planet with other image-bearers (Gen 1:28). God's mission meant he would be glorified by his vice-regents throughout the world. The planet would serve as a temple where people would have intimate fellowship with the Creator without knowing the mediatorial function of a priest. Rather, mankind would be a holy priesthood unto God.

After the fall sin brings judgment, but God's grace brings hope. God stills takes the initiative to come to his creatures, but does so with a message of blessing through judgment (Gen 3:14–15, 21). Relationship will be restored and blessing will come, but atonement must be made for sin. The earth was still to be filled with God's image-bearers (Gen 6:1; 9:1), but the effects of sin would spread throughout the population living on a groaning planet (Rom 8:19–23). Again, a pattern emerges from the Scriptures related to God's purpose in the world: sending → hope through judgment → relationship → blessing.

God takes the initiative to come to his elect, but he does so with a message of hope through judgment. The sin that separates himself from mankind must be addressed. Relationship with God involves a judgment on sin and a faith that brings fellowship. Covenants are cut with the death of animals all foreshadowing the new covenant to come. Mankind and God now enter into relationship through judgment because of sin. But even with judgment, blessings are given and to be enjoyed and used for God's glory. Relationship results in new community with God and his people.

God comes to Moses and sends him to Egypt to deliver Israel from slavery. The message, to both Israel and pharaoh, was that hope would come to God's people, but judgment would come first. Such would befall Egypt, but Israel would have to judge her own sin and be sanctified according to God's plan. The final plague that brought deliverance was only avoided through obedience to God's instructions. At Sinai, God entered into a covenant with his people. They were to be "a kingdom of priests and a holy nation" (Exod

19:6). The covenantal relationship would bring great blessings but also great responsibilities. Israel was to be a light to the nations, pointing God's image-bearers to their Creator who alone was worthy of glory.

Shortly after David becomes king of Israel, God comes to him following this pattern of purpose. The message of hope through judgment is communicated in that David will eventually die, but God will raise up his offspring as part of an eternal kingdom (2 Sam 7:13). Through this Davidic covenant, blessings will come to be enjoyed and used for God's glory.

The long-awaited Davidic descendant would arrive in the fullness of time (Gal 4:4). He was sent to the people of Israel (John 1:14) with a message of hope through judgment. The new covenant in his blood would reveal the full extent of God's judgment on sin and grace and blessing on the nations. As the Father had sent the Son into the world to carry out his purpose, prior to the ascension, the Son would send his disciples to repeat the pattern until he returned.

As the church is sent into the world to encounter image-bearers separated from God, a message of hope through judgment is communicated. People must die to self in repentance toward God and faith in his Messiah (Acts 20:21). Such action brings them into a new kingdom community in which both present and future blessings are a reality (Acts 3:19–20). The pattern of purpose repeats itself as those newly blessed in turn begin to steward well their blessings as they are sent into the world with the message of hope through judgment.

Writing a concise work is both an exciting and daunting task. Whenever one writes an *introductory* book, it is guaranteed that important matters will be omitted due to space considerations. How much more when the author writes a *concise* introduction! Because this book is an overview, I have avoided detailed discussion in areas that some readers will no doubt will find important. For more information, readers should consider the notes and the bibliography.

I am honored to have worked with Todd Hains and the team at Lexham Press on this project. Any shortcomings in the content of this book are my responsibility. I must also offer a word of thanksgiving to Sarah, Hannah, Rachel, and Joel. Their presence and prayers during this project have been my delight. I am so thankful for these four gifts. As always, I am humbled and thankful that the Lord allowed me to produce this text. May it be to his glory!

—J. D. Payne

# CHAPTER 1

# Missional Hermeneutic

THE BIBLE IS comprised of multiple stories that unite to form one grand story revealing God and his mission. In this chapter, I address what a missional hermeneutic is, and how the approach will be advocated throughout this book. As with all forms of biblical interpretation, this method does not escape limitations. However, since God is a God of mission and brings glory to himself, this theme should be prevalent throughout the Scriptures and worthy of consideration.

The entirety of Scripture's story is about mission.[1] This hermeneutic should be granted significant priority because it derives from the unity of the entire canon of Scripture.[2] This approach to interpretation allows the reader to see the beginning, end, and the way between these two points of the biblical storyline. One way to consider this approach to the Scriptures is like a "map," that does not provide "every tiny feature of a landscape," but offers a way to see the entire biblical terrain and how to navigate through it.[3] Comprised of and built from smaller stories, the Bible contains a met-anarrative of the Creator who creates a good creation that is corrupted by the

---

1. N. T. Wright, "The Bible and Christian Mission," in Michael J. Gorman, ed., *Scripture and Its Interpretation: A Global, Ecumenical Introduction to the Bible* (Grand Rapids: Baker Academic, 2017), 397.

2. Harry Daniel Beeby, "A Missional Approach to Renewed Interpretation," in Craig Bartholomew, Colin Greene, and Karl Möller, eds., *Renewing Biblical Interpretation* (Grand Rapids: Zondervan, 2000), 282.

3. Christopher J. H. Wright, "Mission as a Matrix for Hermeneutics and Biblical Theology," in Craig Bartholomew, Mary Healy Karl Möller, eds., *Out of Egypt: Biblical Theology and Biblical Interpretation* (Grand Rapids: Zondervan, 2004), 139.

fall, and who labors to redeem and recreate that which presently groans under the weight of sin.[4]

The Bible was birthed in the context of God carrying out his purpose in the world to redeem a people for himself and restore a groaning creation. The Old Testament was written to a people needing to know the God of Abraham, Isaac, and Jacob. The worldviews of the nations around God's people were significantly distorted by the fall. The ethical practices of the Egyptians, Assyrians, Babylonians, Persians, and other peoples of the ancient Near East fell short of God's expectations. Torah was given to remind Israel where they came from, where they were going, and the need to love God with their entire being (Deut 6:7). God always existed, created everything from nothing, and called Israel to himself so that both Israel and all the nations of the world would be blessed (Gen 12:1–3) and not experience his judgment.

When Israel wandered from Torah, the blessing to her and the nations was at stake. In his grace, God provided prophets to deliver messages calling Israel to covenantal faithfulness. She was to remember what was expected to live with a holy God and repent, or judgment would eventually follow. The cycle of disobedience described in Judges foreshadowed a pattern replicated during the monarchy and following Babylonian exile. Rather than being a "kingdom of priests and a holy nation" (Exod 19:6), that the way of the Lord and his saving power may be known among all nations (Ps 67:3), Israel turned from Torah and became like the nations of the Fertile Crescent. By 587 BC, most of the nation had been destroyed and exiled by Assyrian and Babylonian armies. Israel lost the promised land, the temple, the priesthood and her cultic practices. Jeremiah and other prophets predicted a return to the land and restoration of both Israel and the nations under God's Davidic Servant-King. By the time the Old Testament ends, the political and religious structures are again active in Jerusalem.

The New Testament was also birthed out of the context of God's mission in the world. Neither Jesus nor the first-century disciples saw themselves as a part of a new religious system. They were not plan B, as if Israel thwarted God's mission and he needed to use a backup team. The Gospels

---

4. Richard Bauckham, *Bible and Mission: Christian Witness in a Postmodern World* (Grand Rapids: Baker Books, 2003), 11–12.

are filled with Old Testament prophecies that find their fulfillment in Jesus and the Church's labors. The new covenant addressed in Matthew 26:26–29 takes the reader back to Jeremiah, Isaiah's Suffering Servant, and Exodus's Passover lamb. The arrival of the Spirit at Pentecost (Acts 2) is a fulfillment of Joel's prophecy. The birth and growth of the church, with both Jews and gentiles, was a fulfillment of Amos's prediction of the rebuilding of David's fallen booth (Amos 9:11, 12; Acts 15:16–17).

The letters comprising the New Testament were developed in a context where the Old Testament was the Bible of the people of God. Many of these New Testament writings were written to young churches. The last days had arrived (Acts 2:17) with the day of judgment being the next cosmic event on God's eschatological calendar. However, Jesus commanded his people to preach the gospel and make disciples of all nations before the day arrives (Matt 24:14; 28:18–20). Very soon the nations would be judged, and the restoration of all things would come (Rev 21:1–5). The earth would be filled with God's image-bearers glorifying him and experiencing the fullness of joy and his pleasures forevermore (Ps 16:11).

## A FRESH HERMENEUTIC

A missional hermeneutic is a means of interpreting the Scriptures, in their historical and cultural contexts, with the person and work of Christ and the mission of God as the central key to proper understanding of the biblical story.[5] While it is assumed by some to be primarily observed in the New Testament, the key of messiah and mission is quite evident throughout the Old Testament as well. This interpretative approach must reflect the whole canon of Scripture, clarify what is at stake, and articulate the Bible's message.[6] A missional hermeneutic is the result of recognizing God's mission in the canon of Scripture.[7]

This mission-centered approach to reading the Bible has not always been the case, and it still remains foreign to many readers. However, in the later twentieth and early-twenty first centuries, scholars began to advocate

---

5. For an evaluation of four different approaches to a missional hermeneutic see George R. Hunsberger, "Proposals for a Missional Hermeneutic: Mapping a Conversation," in *Missiology* 39, no. 3 (July 2011): 309–21.

6. Wright, "Mission as a Matrix for Hermeneutics and Biblical Theology," 138.

7. Wright, "Mission as a Matrix for Hermeneutics and Biblical Theology," 122.

this approach to biblical interpretation. At the turn of the century, Harry Daniel Beeby expressed his concerns with present-day hermeneutics and offered the following as a prescription for the problem:

> I believe that biblical understanding, investigation, reading and usage are in crisis; that the questions and the problems that face us are almost beyond numbering but that among all the approaches to be made there is one, rarely considered, which is so important that renewal will fail if it continues to be neglected. The approach is of those who read in the Bible the account of the *missio Dei* and who believe that it provides a trajectory essential to full hermeneutical renewal.[8]

While a missional hermeneutic is not as widespread as desired, it has experienced growth over the past two decades. If Beeby's crisis remains, then what can be done? One response is missiologists and theologians need to communicate with each other. Scholars in these two disciplines have at times kept their worlds separated.[9] This dichotomy often resulted in biblical and theological studies focusing on the church itself, while viewing mission as a stepchild. Missiologists lacking serious biblical study often turned to oversimplification and prooftexting.[10] Textual diversity and historical character, sometimes with little attention to contemporary relevance, have been the concerns of many biblical scholars, while missiologists have overlooked these important matters to fall into the unhealthy pit of eisegesis.[11] While I cannot guarantee this book will completely avoid these concerns, I shall work diligently to avoid them in an attempt to bring the theological and missiological realms together regarding mission as a biblical and theological theme.

---

8. Beeby, "Missional Approach to Renewed Interpretation," 268.

9. Beeby, "Missional Approach to Renewed Interpretation," 278.

10. Charles R. Taber, "Missiology and the Bible," *Missiology* 11, no. 2 (April 1983): 229–230.

11. Johannes Nissen, *New Testament and Missions: Historical and Hermeneutical Perspectives*, 3rd ed. (Frankfurt: Peter Lang, 2004), 13.

## BIBLICAL-THEOLOGICAL APPROACH

A missional hermeneutic is not a panacea. Following this paradigm will not resolve all interpretive challenges found in the Old and New Testaments.[12] There is a great amount of diversity in the Bible: different genres, writing styles, grammatical expressions, emphases, and themes, as well as writing locations and historical contextual event. [13] Yet, within this diversity, there is great unity, especially for those who believe that the Bible, in its entirety, is God's revelation to his people.[14]

I am aware scholarship has problems not only discussing unity within either the Old or New Testament books, but even the relationship of these two volumes to one another is seriously questioned.[15] It is beyond the scope of this introductory book to enter into an apologetic regarding the details of the scholarly debates on this relationship. There is much internal evidence, when subjected to scholarship and reason, that reveals unifying threads woven throughout the sixty-six books of the Bible. One of these unifiers is the significant thread of God's mission.

If the sovereign God is true to his character, then he is able to allow for healthy diversity and unity to coexist in his Scriptures. Consider van Gogh's portfolio or Mozart's symphonic repertoire. Their works were created over lifetimes. They display variations based on the periods of their compositions. However, the stylistic aspects of each artist run throughout their works. It is possible to extract their creations, at any moment in their careers, and observe the unifying stylistic features in view of diversity and change. If God is a God of mission, then this aspect of his nature and functions should be found across the pages of biblical revelation.[16]

---

12. John Goldingay, *Theological Diversity and the Authority of the Old Testament* (Grand Rapids: Eerdmans, 1987), viii.

13. Lucien Legrand, *Unity and Plurality: Mission in the Bible*, English translation by Robert R. Barr (Maryknoll, NY: Orbis Books, 1990), 7.

14. H. D. Beeby spends a great deal of time addressing the canon, unity, diversity, and mission in his work *Canon and Mission* (Harrisburg, PA: Trinity Press International, 1999).

15. For more on this topic see David Baker, *Two Testaments, One Bible*.

16. Taber, 231. David Filbeck describes the "missionary dimension" as that which "unifies both the Old and New Testament" and "coordinates their various themes into a single motif." See David Filbeck, *Yes, God of the Gentiles, Too: The Missionary Message of the Old Testament* (Wheaton, IL: Billy Graham Center, 1994), 10.

## CHRISTOCENTRIC-MISSIONAL APPROACH

The Bible begins with God's dealings with the nations and concludes with God's concern with the nations. God's purposes related to the nations form the basic story of Scripture.[17] The first century believers read the Old Testament from a historical, messianic, and kingdom perspective. Torah, Prophets, and Writings were God's revelation to his people and relevant for their day. As will be shown, the early disciples often returned to the Scriptures (and thus Israel's history) to find explanation, support, and guidance for contemporary works of the Spirit. Jesus did not come to abolish the Law or the Prophets, but to fulfill them (Matt 5:17). He had no problem revealing how the Scriptures pointed to himself (Luke 24:27, 44). Following the resurrection and ascension, the disciples believed Jesus was the Messiah sent from the God of Abraham, Isaac, and Jacob. He came and fulfilled parts of his mission as it was not the time for the kingdom to be fully restored (Acts 1:6-7). The great restoration would arrive, but in the interim, the divine mission remained. The disciples were to bear witness to the Savior starting in Jerusalem (Acts 1:8) and establish kingdom communities throughout the world that would live out the kingdom ethic until the parousia.[18]

A missional hermeneutic attempts to draw from this interpretative framework of the first century believers. A christological and missiological reading of the Bible does not mean Jesus or missionary activity are found in every passage. However, some passages, in their historic contexts, address the Messiah and mission in more detail than others. History shows it is possible to have a high view of the Messiah and commit the fallacy of eisegesis in his name. A missional hermeneutic is not about stretching the text to mean something it was never intended to mean; rather, a missional hermeneutic is governed by a christological pivot.[19]

A missional hermeneutic is not about prooftexting to feign the appearance of Jesus and mission. Prooftexting may draw attention to significant passages related to the desired outcome, but it avoids addressing passages that offer little support to (or conflict with) the overall metanarrative of the

---

17. Charles H. H. Scobie, "Israel and the Nations: An Essay in Biblical Theology," *Tyndale Bulletin* 43, no. 2 (1992): 285.

18. See Wright, "The Bible and Christian Mission," 388.

19. Wright, "The Bible and Christian Mission."

Bible. It is appealing, but dishonest. This book attempts to avoid this problem, recognizing portions of the Old and New Testaments may have little direct bearing on the topic. Some of the important sub-themes addressed will receive less attention than others.

While this hermeneutic is used to understand the "then and there" of the biblical stories, it is also applied to asking about the relevance to the "here and now" of those same stories.[20] Orthodoxy is meant to transition into kingdom service. This is especially true in the area of disciple making. The mission of God belongs to God, but the Scriptures come with the expectation that the people of God will engage with his mission.[21] The aforementioned pattern of sending and proclaiming a message of hope through judgment is a significant part of the church's apostolic work in the world.

## CONCLUSION

A missional hermeneutic is used throughout this book. Messiah and mission is a key to understanding the biblical storyline. While the Bible contains a great wealth of diversity, such is not a problem to understanding God's work in the *cosmos*. Diversity should be expected, given the epochs, genres, settings, and characters encountered. However, within diversity there is continuity and unity. The character and actions of God are consistent throughout the Scriptures. Before beginning with a study of mission in Torah, it is necessary to turn attention to the God who sends.

---

20. Gordon D. Fee and Douglas Stuart popularized this language regarding exegesis and hermeneutics in their book *How to Read the Bible for All Its Worth: A Guide to Understanding the Bible* (Grand Rapids: Zondervan, 1981).

21. Robert L. Plummer, *Paul's Understanding of the Church's Mission: Did the Apostle Paul Expect the Early Christian Communities to Evangelize?* (Eugene, OR: Wipf & Stock, 2006).

## REFLECTION QUESTIONS

1.  How would you define missional hermeneutic in your own words?

2.  What does it mean to read the Bible from a christological and missiological perspective? Do you read the Bible this way? If not, how would you describe your approach?

3.  How does knowing the New Testament was birthed in the context of the church carrying out the purpose of God affect the way you will read it in the future?

# CHAPTER 2

# The God Who Sends

T HE BIBLICAL STORYLINE reveals a God who remains faithful to his promises which require the ongoing sending of himself and his servants into a tragically suffering and deeply needy world to accomplish his mission of redemption and restoration. Mission begins in the heart of God and flows from his nature. He is glorified through relationship with the nations and extending his blessing to them. He reveals himself as deeply concerned with a divine plan, his plan, a plan that existed in eternity past. His work involves the election of the saints "before the foundation of the world" (Eph 1:4; cf. Rev 13:8) and the sacrifice and exaltation of the Son (1 Pet 1:20). His plan comes with a strategy. An objective, even within the heart of God, requires action. God is there and working his will (John 14:10). Mission began with God, is sustained by God, and will culminate with God. Mission is not an activity developed by the church; rather, the church participates in God's mission. Mission belongs to him.

God's strategic plan for executing his mission begins with the concept of *sent*. For example, the New Testament's use of the verb *apostello* ("send") from which the noun *apostolos* ("apostle") is derived reveals the connection between God's work in the world and his messengers. Sending is necessary for mission. Jesus is called an apostle (Heb 3:1) and sent to do the work of the Lord (Luke 4:18). Jesus calls his disciples and sends them to preach (Mark 3:14). Paul recognized himself to be called an apostle and set apart for the gospel work (Rom 1:1).

During the late twentieth century, Francis M. DuBose published *God Who Sends: A Fresh Quest for Biblical Mission*. This work was the first book-length study (at least in English) of the biblical concept of sending. The title was selected "because God as Sender is the basis of all the Bible has to say on the subject."[1] While the church has often understood sending in view of Jesus being sent from the Father (John 3:17), or Jesus sending his disciples in light of the Great Commission (Matt 28:19; John 20:21), the Scriptures root this apostolic act with the God who creates and sends himself into his creation.[2] Since his interest in redeeming the world and extending that glory existed long before the first century, it is important to recognize mission did not begin at Pentecost. Before venturing into an examination of the different sections of the Bible, our journey begins in this chapter by obtaining an overview of God's apostolic (i.e., sending) nature.

## IN THE BEGINNING ... GOD SENT HIMSELF

The story of the Bible begins with a God who steps out of infinity and eternity and creates the finite (Gen 1:5) in time (Gen 1:14). Though the writer does not reveal the divine motives for such actions, God moves to accomplish this act and develop the results. From the beginning, God is intimately involved with the creation process as his Spirit broods over the waters like a hen waiting for an egg to hatch (Gen 1:2).

God is described as speaking throughout the creation account. "And God said," or "God called," is the refrain of Genesis 1. The reader immediately realizes this God is not simply a transcendent deity, but also an imminent being who communicates in such a way that the cosmos responds to his will. Man and woman (Gen 1:28–30; 2:16–17) hear him speak and understand his language. After the fall, such knowledge becomes critical to the redemptive process. Unless people are able to hear and understand the message of hope through judgment, relationship with God is non-existent.

God sends himself into time and space and communes with his creation. He assigned Adam and Eve tasks and explained how they were to live on the earth. When the man and woman hide themselves from God walking

---

1. Francis M. DuBose, *God Who Sends: A Fresh Quest for Biblical Mission* (Nashville: Broadman & Holman, 1983), 7.

2. Robert Martin-Achard describes mission as "a theocentric concept in the sense that is brought into being and put into effect by God Himself and at the same time furthers His glory." *A Light to the Nations: A Study of the Old Testament Conception of Israel's Mission to the World*, English ed. (Edinburgh: Oliver & Boyd, 1962), 76.

the garden (Gen 3:8), it is because of their sin and shame, not because they were shocked God would visit them. They had been used to such intimacy with him. In all likelihood God had been visiting the garden in the cool of the day to be with Adam and Eve on previous occasions. From the beginning, they and their descendants, divine image-bearers, were to walk in such fellowship with God throughout the earth and enjoy his blessings (Gen 1:28). Here is an important point to grasp: *God's mission has always been to have the earth filled with his people* (Isa 45:18). Genesis 1:28 was not only a pre-fall expectation. Following Noah's departure from the ark, Moses records (twice) the command to multiply and fill the earth (9:1, 7).

The grace of the apostolic God is clearly revealed after the fall. While he was under no obligation to engage the couple, he does just that. True to his word, he arrives and states the consequences of the trespasses. Within this dark moment in history, God announces the good news of hope through judgment that the seed of the woman will crush the head of the serpent (Gen 3:15). This early account shows God's mission already, as he comes to Adam and Eve to address sin, a reflection of the gospel.[3]

God came to Adam and Eve with a message of hope through judgment. Suffering, separation, hardships, and death are now present. Yet, a day will come when the serpent will be overthrown. Until that time of blessing, God will still bless his people. Adam and Eve are clothed and will still be able to multiply and fill the earth. Though sent from the garden, as God's image-bearers, they were to continue to bring glory to him (Gen 3:23-24). This model of sending → message → relationship → blessing will become a pattern throughout the Bible. People (Jew and gentile) will rebel against God. They will suffer for their sins, but he will move to them and bring a means of redemption and restoration.

## I WILL MAKE YOU A GREAT NATION
## … YOU WILL BE A BLESSING

As the effects of the fall multiplied throughout the earth (Gen 6:1, 5), God began to relate to people through covenant. His message of hope through judgment came to Noah, who found grace in God's eyes (Gen 6:8; 9:8-17). Noah, his family, and the animals were spared from judgment (Gen 7:21-23).

---

3. See DuBose, *God Who Sends*, 57.

Yet, the sin nature remained with this family. After returning to land, both people and evil multiplied. Following the Table of Nations (Gen 10) and the Babel incident (Gen 11), the record notes how the line of Shem eventually results in the birth of Abraham (Gen 11:10–26). And it is at this point of the biblical storyline that the call of Abraham offers more clarity to how God's mission will bring hope to a world filled with sin. Abraham is elected by God to be used as a blessing to all the nations (Gen 12:1–3).[4] More will be stated regarding God's covenant with Abraham in the next chapter. For now, we need to understand the movement of God toward this man brought *both* blessings and responsibilities.[5]

Torah continues with God's movement toward his people for his task. Early in Exodus, he sends himself to Moses (3:1–12) to reveal a plan of deliverance for his people from Egypt. Some have seen Moses as a missionary.[6] Exodus through Joshua develops the theme of God's mission in the world as the promise to Abraham manifests through a large number of descendants, the Mosaic covenant, priesthood, tabernacle, and the reception of the promised land.

In the Prophets, God sends himself to David and enters into a covenant (2 Sam 7:1–16). Though David wanted to build God a house, God comes and promises to build David an eternal dynasty. Among other details, the promise involved an heir always seated on David's throne. Israel eventually turns her back on God and suffers for her sins. Prior to the Babylonian captivity, God sent himself to prophets to foretell that Israel would return to the land (Jer 29:14). She would receive a new covenant (Jer 31:31–34) and a righteous, Davidic Shepherd-king (Mic 5:2–5). Her destroyed temple would be rebuilt, and the glory of the Second Temple would dwarf that of the first (Hag 2:9). God's people would be filled with his Spirit (Joel 2:28–29), and during the last days, God would move the nations to Jerusalem to know him and

---

4. Paul returns to this account to note "the Scripture, foreseeing that God would justify the Gentiles by faith, preached the gospel beforehand to Abraham" (Gal 3:8). We will examine the Pauline writings in a later chapter. For now, note the importance of this passage in Paul's thought.

5. Henry Cornell Goerner, *Thus It is Written: The Missionary Motif in the Scriptures* (Nashville: Broadman & Holman, 1944), 6.

6. H. H. Rowley, *The Missionary Message of the Old Testament* (London: The Carey Kingsgate Press, 1944), 15. Most scholars would disagree with Rowley's claim that "Moses was the first missionary of whom we have any knowledge."

Torah (Mic 4:1–2). The thread of the mission of God is woven throughout the Old Testament. Torah, Prophets, and the Writings will be examined in subsequent chapters.

## THE WORD WAS SENT

The writer of the Fourth Gospel saw the connection between the sending nature of God entering into contact with his creation and the fulfillment of the Edenic promise of the crushing of the serpent. Though Moses was sent from God to lead the Israelites, it was God who came to dwell in the center of the camp as his presence filled the tabernacle (Exod 40:34–38). John's language draws from Old Testament terminology and images when he writes "the Word, became flesh and dwelt [i.e., tabernacled] among us" (John 1:14). While the presence of the Baptist caused some to wonder if he were the Christ (1:20), John made it clear the Baptist was sent from God (1:6) and pointed to the Lamb who takes away the sins of the world (1:29). This Jesus was sent from God, not to condemn the world, but to save it (John 3:17). Hope, blessing, and relationship would come, but judgment was necessary as the Lamb would be slain.

## SENT AS MY WITNESSES

The fulfillment of Joel's prophecy (Joel 2:28–32) in Acts 2 was a significant moment on God's eschatological calendar. Before the day of the Lord, God would send his Spirit on his people (Joel 2:28; Acts 2:17). While Luke notes Peter was the one to connect the Pentecostal experience to the prophet, the apostles knew the Son promised the Spirit to provide comfort, instruction, guidance (John 14:16, 26), and power (Acts 1:8) for the global task of making disciples (Matt 28:18–20; John 15:26–27).

The presence of God transitioned from walking with Adam in the garden, dwelling among Israel in the tabernacle and temple, abiding among Israel as the Nazarene, to now filling everyone who calls upon the name of the Lord. The nations were no longer expected to travel to Mount Zion to hear the word of the Lord. The community of God's people under the Messiah are the royal priesthood and holy nation (1 Pet 2:9), the temple, and filled with the Spirit (1 Cor 3:16–17). They are empowered and sent to the nations by the Father, Son, and Spirit (Luke 24:49; John 20:21).

The theology of mission must discuss the Trinitarian work of the Father, Son, and Spirit.[7] This proclamation, sharing, and bearing is manifested throughout the book of Acts and the rest of the New Testament.

Acts 1:8 foreshadows what is to unfold throughout the book. The disciples carry the gospel wherever they go. As they share the good news, some people believe while others do not. The unrepentant frequently respond to the proclamation with opposition. The life shared and witness expressed moves from Jerusalem to the ends of the earth, frequently breaking through cultural barriers as the kingdom of God expands (Acts 8; 10; 11; 13–14; 28). Though opposition arises from inside and outside the faith community, and believers are killed and imprisoned, the proclamation of the kingdom of God and his Christ continues "with all boldness and without hindrance" (Acts 28:31).

The Pauline and General Epistles address challenges related to these young kingdom communities that have been the recipients of the good news sent to them via God's messengers. Their relationship with God brought blessings to be enjoyed and used for his purpose in the world. Revelation concludes the biblical storyline with people from every tribe, language, and nation represented in the kingdom (Rev 7:9–10; 22:3–5). The Messiah will be sent once again, but will bring judgment and usher in the restoration of all things (Rev 19:11–16; 21). God's image-bearers will fill the near heaven and earth, delighting in his blessings and glorifying him forever. God's work of redemption and restoration will be complete.

Before journeying through the Bible and considering the work of the God who sends, a few technical concepts need to be addressed. When speaking of God's purpose in the world, scholars have used four specific terms. Particularity and universality help explain the work of God in relation to the few in order to bless the many. Centripetal and centrifugal describe the movements of the nations to the people of God and the people of God to the nations.

---

7. For a discussion of the role of each person of the Trinity in mission, see Lesslie Newbigin, *The Open Secret: An Introduction to the Theology of Mission*, rev. ed. (Grand Rapids: Eerdmans, 1995), 29.

## UNIVERSALITY AND PARTICULARITY

God desires to bless the nations (universality), but he works through an elect people (particularity) to accomplish this mission.[8] Scholars have described this as a tension, even a perceived conflict. While such may be the case, an unhealthy tension does not exist. Both are necessary for the mission of God in the world.

The Bible begins with God blessing the many represented by the first family of all of creation. Soon the effects of the fall and the multiplication of sin increase and spread. Yet even at this point in the story, the godly line of those who "call upon the name of the Lord" (Gen 4:26) are represented by Seth and his descendants down to Noah. Following the flood, the narrative traces the line of Shem to Terah and then Abraham (Gen 11:10–32). Though Terah and Abraham served other gods (Josh 24:2), something was unique regarding the descendants of Seth and God's mission to bless all nations.

When we are introduced to Abraham, the focus of the line of blessing becomes very specific (particularism). Throughout the rest of the Bible, God's blessings will come to all people (universality) through the children of Abraham (particularity). This continues in the New Testament, for the true children of Abraham are those of faith (Gal 3:7).

When God elects Israel (in Abraham) to be his people, he is not showing a rejection of the nations. Rather, this amazing privilege comes with a tremendous responsibility on behalf of the nations.[9] Election does not entail self-glorification, but calls the elect into a life of service to the world for God's glorification.[10]

---

8. Some scholars choose to use the words universalism and particularism.

9. Johannes Blauw, *The Missionary Nature of the Church: A Survey of the Biblical Theology of Mission* (New York: McGraw-Hill, 1962), 23, 25.

10. Rowley, *The Missionary Message of the Old Testament*, 58. Martin-Achard also draws attention to the universal blessing of God being related to his particular blessing to Abraham: "The ultimate destiny of the world depends on the existence of Israel in the midst of the nations; in living by Yahweh the Chosen People lives for mankind." *A Light to the Nations*, 31.

## CENTRIPETAL AND CENTRIFUGAL

The methods by which God extends his universal blessings to all peoples via his chosen people has been described by the words centripetal and centrifugal.[11] The centripetal method is understood as the drawing of the nations to Israel, particularly to the temple in Jerusalem. This is the primary means by which many scholars understand Israel's relationship to God's mission and the nations in the Old Testament. Israel lives as God's holy nation and priests, and the peoples are *drawn* to such blessing and awe of Israel's God. Many scholars agree this is the means by which Israel is engaged in *missions* in the Old Testament. Instead of being *sent*, she walks faithfully with God, attracting the nations to him.[12] The universal blessing arrives when the nations come to him through this particular people.

The centrifugal method is observed in the New Testament. The people of God are sent to the nations with the good news of the kingdom. A methodological shift occurs between the Old and New Testaments. Instead of the nations being drawn to God and his people like the Queen of Sheba (1 Kgs 10:1), Naaman (2 Kgs 5:1–14) and the Ethiopian (Acts 8:26–28), the church is sent to the nations. The universal blessing arrives when the particular people take the good news to the nations.

While this dichotomy of methodology has been accepted for many years among scholars, this understanding is reductionistic. While the overwhelming evidence in the Old Testament points to a centripetal paradigm, there are at least three examples of the centrifugal paradigm in place. Jonah is sent to the Ninevites with a message of judgment. While his attitude and actions are hardly a model for apostolic work, he was sent to represent YHWH and bring the message that would lead to the averting of judgment.[13] Elijah was sent to the widow of Zarephath to receive care, but

---

11. The origin of the centripetal and centrifugal thinking is traced to the work of Bengt Sundkler, "Jésus et les Païens," in *Revue d'histoire et de Philosophie Religieuses* (Novembre–Décembre 1936): 462–99.

12. Walter C. Kaiser, Jr., however, argues Israel had a mandate to go to the nations with Torah. See Walter C. Kaiser, Jr. *Mission in the Old Testament: Israel as a Light to the Nations*, 2nd ed. (Grand Rapids: Baker Academic, 2012).

13. It should be noted that not all scholars agree Jonah is an example of the centrifugal paradigm.

also so he could reveal God's mercy to her and her son (1 Kgs 17:8–24).[14] The other example is found in Isaiah 66 when God sends his people to "declare my glory among the nations" (66:19). These two examples foreshadow what is expected of God's people in the New Testament and not an expected model for Israel in the Old Testament.[15]

It is even more problematic to define the New Testament paradigm in purely centrifugal terms. The church is to live out the kingdom ethic so others may see the good works and glorify God (Matt 5:14–16; 1 Pet 3:1–4). As the temple of the Holy Spirit, God's people are not only going to the nations, but the nations are being pulled to this new expression of the temple.[16]

## CONCLUSION

Understanding mission requires that we recognize God as both sender and sent.[17] This characteristic of God's nature is found throughout the Bible and significant for our study. Without God's initiative, there is no mission, and thus no relationship and blessing among his image-bearers. God's mission in the Old Testament is dynamically connected to his presence in creation as he comes to Abraham, Moses, Israel, and David. The universal blessing of God would extend to the nations as they were to be drawn to him through his particular people. His sending nature continues to manifest itself in the New Testament. God the Father sends God the Son into the world. The Son sends the twelve and the seventy-two throughout Israel and then to the nations. The Father and the Son send the Spirit. The Spirit sends the

---

14. Jesus also drew attention to Elijah being sent to her and not to a widow of God's chosen people (Luke 4:24–27). His point was Israel had a history of rejecting God's messengers, and he would go beyond Nazareth. The wrath of the people was raised when it was noted God had a history of accomplishing His mission though receptive gentiles.

15. Dean Flemming also believes Jonah, while "not intended to be a paradigm for Israel's missionary outreach," foreshadows the church's calling to the nations. See Dean Flemming, *Recovering the Full Mission of God: A Biblical Perspective on Being, Doing and Telling* (Downers Grove, IL: IVP Academic, 2013), 47.

16. Even the church's worship gathering possibly expressed the centripetal effect (1 Cor 14:24–25). Some scholars argue the centrifugal method of the New Testament will shift back to a centripetal model in the eschaton when the nations will stream to Zion. See Craig Ott, Stephen J. Strauss, with Timothy C. Tennent, *Encountering Theology of Mission: Biblical Foundations, Historical Developments, and Contemporary Issues* (Grand Rapids: Baker Academic, 2010), 53.

17. Georg F. Vicedom, *The Mission of God: An Introduction to a Theology of Mission* (St. Louis: Concordia, 1965), 7.

church into the world. The Son is sent to earth at the parousia. But for now, it is necessary to begin by considering some of the sub-themes related to the mission of God in Torah.

## REFLECTION QUESTIONS

1. How does knowing that God sent himself into creation (e.g., Eden, Bethlehem) influence the way you think about God's mission in your life? Church? World?

2. Do you think Israel had a mandate to go to the nations with Torah? Why?

3. How is your church practicing both centripetal and centrifugal methods to mission?

# CHAPTER 3

# Mission in Torah

THOUGH THE OLD Testament was the Bible of Jesus and the first-century apostles, it is easy for Christians to give little attention to this portion of the Scriptures when it comes to God's work in the world.[1] The church is often quick to jump to the Great Commission texts of Matthew 28:18–20 and Acts 1:8 for a foundation for apostolic labors. However, the basis of her mission is found in the Old Testament beginning with Torah.[2]

Overlooking the mission of God in these books is detrimental to a biblical understanding of the functions of the church in both the first century and our time as well. The life, ministry, death, and resurrection of Jesus Christ do not nullify the mighty acts and words of God in Abraham and his seed.[3]

The Pentateuch develops the subtheme of God's image-bearers filling the world. While the majority of the world wanders away from his relationship and blessings, the particularity of God's mission is developed with the story that traces a godly line of Adam through Seth to Noah and then to Abraham and Israel. The people of God enter into relationship with him and experience his blessings by faith. Throughout these five books, God's glory among the nations comes through three particular means: 1) Through a Person: Abraham; 2) Through a People: Israel; and 3) Through a Place: Tabernacle.

---

1. See J. Robertson McQuilkin, "An Evangelical Assessment of Mission Theology of the Kingdom of God," in Charles Van Engen, Dean S. Gilliland, and Paul Pierson, eds., *The Good News of the Kingdom: Mission Theology for the Third Millennium* (Maryknoll, NY: Orbis Books, 1993), 176.

2. Johannes Blauw, *The Missionary Nature of the Church: A Survey of the Biblical Theology of Mission* (New York: McGraw-Hill, 1962), 15.

3. Dean Flemming, *Recovering the Full Mission of God: A Biblical Perspective on Being, Doing and Telling* (Downers Grove, IL: IVP Academic, 2013), 57.

## BLESSING THE NATIONS: CREATED
## IN THE IMAGE OF GOD

God is without creation. Yet, he creates everything that exists. He is self-sufficient and shown from the beginning to be intimately connected to his created order (Gen 1:1–2). He did not need the earth, animals, or humans. Within his plan, the creation of such was the route to bring him the most glory. Genesis records everything was created in six days with God resting on the seventh day. At various times throughout the creation narrative, Moses notes that God's acts were recognized as good (1:10, 12, 18, 21, 25). God is not subject to the sun, other stars, or the moon. Rather, he creates them with the practical function of light and time keeping (Gen 1:14–19). Such heavenly bodies are not divine, nor do they influence the destinies of people. Everything that exists is visualized, organized, and operationalized by himself. Only one God exists, and the cosmos has no dominion over him or his image-bearers.[4]

God's reflection following the creation of man and woman brought about the understanding that what he made was "very good" (1:31). On the sixth day, he created man and woman in his own image (1:27). They were given dominion over the earth, blessed by God, and commanded to "be fruitful and multiply and fill the earth and subdue it" (1:28). The first couple was engaged in work that involved caring for Eden and naming the living creatures (2:15; 19). G. K. Beale refers to Genesis 1:28 as the "first Great Commission." While his terminology is unusual, his point is clear:

> The commission was to bless the earth, and part of the essence of this blessing was God's salvific presence. Before the fall, Adam and Eve were to produce progeny who would fill the earth with God's glory being reflected from each of them in the image of God. After the fall, a remnant, created by God in his restored image, were to go out and spread God's glorious presence among the rest of darkened humanity. This "witness" was to continue until the entire world would be filled with divine glory.[5]

---

4. See Gordon J. Wenham, *Genesis 1–15* (Dallas: Word, 1998), xlvii.

5. G. K. Beale, *The Temple and the Church's Mission: A Biblical Theology of the Dwelling Place of God* (Leicester, UK: Apollos, 2004), 117–18.

As God's image-bearers procreated and migrated, the uninhabited planet would be filled with people delighting in God and his blessings. Centuries later, the prophet would write that God created the earth and "formed it to be inhabited" (Isa 45:18). People were to bring glory to God through fellowship with him (3:8), healthy relationships with one another and the created order, and the establishment of civilization and culture.[6] The entire earth was designed to be a planetary temple, filled with God's glory (Num 14:21; Ps 72:19; Isa 6:3).[7]

The rebellion of the first couple resulted in sin entering into the world. The woman now experiences pain during childbirth, the couple's relationship is strained at times, and the man's work fails to produce the desired results with ease (Gen 3:16–19). While humans were created to live forever in fellowship with God, a day would come when the breath of life would be removed from them (Gen 3:19). The blessings of God will often become idols that result in broken fellowship and judgment. The world that was to be received with great delight now groans under the weight of sin (Rom 8:19–23). The cultivation and dominion of the earth will come with great struggle and problems. Caring for the created order will often result in its desecration and destruction. Sin brings judgment and consequences.

It is in this dark narrative that the reader encounters a grand, glorious, and mysterious promise. In God's curse upon the serpent, a day will come when the offspring of the woman will deliver a death blow to the creature's head. Through judgment, hope is found. Her seed will be harmed but victorious over the deceiver (Gen 3:15). This first announcement of the good news shows up very early in the biblical narrative. As the glory of Eden was quickly ruined, God quickly sends himself into the dark garden to bring the light of good news and care for the couple in their sin and shame (Gen 3:21).

The story continues with the reader wondering when this seed of the woman would destroy the serpent. While hope is stirred in chapter four with the birth of Cain, the reader quickly discovers that he is a murderer, and righteous Abel is killed. Hope arises again in chapter five with the birth of Seth and his descendants, for it was during the days of Seth's first

---

6. It is worth noting that the command was repeated following the fall (Gen 9:1).

7. The concept of the earth being a temple is developed extensively in the work of G. K. Beale. For his treatment on the place of the temple in God's mission, see *The Temple and the Church's Mission*.

child "people began to call upon the name of the Lord" (Gen 4:26). However, with each addition to Adam and Eve's family tree, the author includes the refrain that the person lived a certain number of years "and he died." While Enoch walked with God, he was not the one to destroy the serpent (Gen 5:22). Lamech made a prediction about his son Noah, noting he "shall bring us relief from our work and from the painful toil of our hands" (Gen 5:29). Noah indeed finds favor in the eyes of the Lord (Gen 6:8) and escapes the flood (Gen 7; cf. Heb 11:7).

Following the deluge, God makes a covenant with Noah, his descendants, and every living creature (Gen 8:20–9:17). Though "the intention of man's heart is evil from his youth" (Gen 8:21), God will never again destroy all living creatures by water. This is a significant development in the story of God's mission in the world.[8] At this point, the reader may be asking, "Since God has reset everything to the time of a single family and the animals, does this mean that righteousness will overcome evil?" But just after such a question may be raised, Genesis immediately reveals the effects of the curse have not been removed from the earth among Noah's family (Gen 9:20–29). Sin and its multifaceted repercussions spread. God continues to work. His mission remains.

The Table of Nations in Genesis 10 lists the descendants of Noah and his family. Rather than this account being a genealogical record to be glossed over, it shows God's universal concern for the nations. Humankind is one and created by one God.[9] In the Table, Israel is represented in the genes of Shem and his descendants, which includes several non-outstanding characters.[10]

If placing lackluster characters alongside the rest of the nations were not sufficient to illustrate Israel's common origin, the call of Abraham would serve as a clear reminder. He was from the land of the Chaldeans

8. Peter J. Gentry and Stephen J. Wellum, *Kingdom through Covenant: A Biblical-Theological Understanding of the Covenants* (Wheaton, IL: Crossway, 2012), 175. Gentry and Wellum's tome is a significant work that attempts to examine the covenants in their historical-textual contexts and then view them intertextually and canonically to understand the whole counsel of God. I will direct the reader to their excellent work (now in 2nd edition), for such details about the covenants are beyond the scope of this concise theology.

9. Robert Martin-Achard, *A Light to the Nations: A Study of the Old Testament Conception of Israel's Mission to the World* (Edinburgh: Oliver & Boyd, 1962), 36.

10. For a discussion of the significance of the people and nations named, see Arthur F. Glasser, *Announcing the Kingdom: The Story of God's Mission in the Bible* (Grand Rapids: Baker Academic, 2003), 51.

(Gen 11:28, 31), and described by Joshua as one who served other gods (Josh 24:2). Israel's ancestors were no different than the other nations of the Fertile Crescent. Because God was concerned for all of them, he sent himself to Abraham.

But before examining the Abrahamic covenant in God's mission, Genesis 11:1–9 provides an important element to the story of God's mission in the world and people's rebellion. As the population multiplies, people migrate until some groups desire to cease their travels and make a name for themselves. Their actions are described as an act of defiance to God's command to multiply and fill the earth (Gen 11:4). They want nothing to do with God or his mission in the world. The result of their decisions in the land of Shinar caused the Lord to confuse their language and scatter them across the earth (Gen 11:9). Here is a reoccurring theme that shows up throughout the Scriptures. Numerous attempts are made, from various parties at various times, to stop God's mission. The result is always the same: God's mission in the world continues. The tower of Babel was no exception, but served as a foreshadowing of things to come throughout both the Old and New Testaments.

## BLESSING THE NATIONS THROUGH A PERSON: ABRAHAM

Genesis 12:1–3 is a significant moment in the history of God's work in the world. The means to destroy the serpent and restoration all things is clarified with the introduction of Abraham.[11] His origins are limited to a few verses. We know he was a descendant of Noah's son, Shem. His father was Terah. He lived in Ur and was married to Sarah. Abraham and his family moved and settled in the land of Haran, where Terah died (Gen 11:32). Sarah is introduced as a woman who "was barren" (Gen 11:30). This initial impression is more than a stigma borne by Abraham's wife. It serves to emphasize the miracle that God was about do through this family.

> Now the LORD said to Abram, "Go from your country and your kindred and your father's house to the land that I will show you. And I will make of you a great nation, and I will bless you and make your

---

11. His original name was Abram, and his wife, Sarai.

name great, so that you will be a blessing. I will bless those who bless you, and him who dishonors you I will curse, and in you all the families of the earth shall be blessed." (Gen 12:1–3)

The call of Abraham marks the beginning of the history of Israel. God was going to bless the nations by electing a specific people to come from Abraham and Sarah.[12] From the beginning, Israel's history is intimately connected to God's relationship to the nations.[13] Why did God call Abraham to himself and promise to bless him, curse those who curse him, give him a great name, and make him (and his barren wife) into a great nation? The writer avoids all equivocation as to the reason: "so that you will be a blessing," and "in you all the families of the earth shall be blessed."[14]

It is worth noting both God's initiative and responsibility in this call and promise to Abraham. It is God who takes the initiative and comes to Abraham. The patriarch's election had nothing to do with godly actions. As Joshua later reminds Israel of her history, he writes, "Long ago, your fathers lived beyond the Euphrates, Terah, the father of Abraham and of Nahor; and they served other gods" (Josh 24:2). Next, the number of times God states, in such a few verses, what he will do to bless Abraham is astounding. The onus is on God, and he places it there himself.

Before we assume Abraham, and thus Israel, was to be passive in the Lord's work, it is important to recognize election is both a privilege and responsibility.[15] Israel (i.e., Abraham) was chosen to be God's people for a

---

12. For now, it is worth noting that God's relationship with Abraham receives much attention in the New Testament. Citing Genesis 12:3, Paul claims this is a reference to the gospel: "And the Scripture, foreseeing that God would justify the gentiles by faith, preached the gospel beforehand to Abraham, saying, 'In you shall all the nations be blessed'" (Gal 3:8).

13. Blauw, *The Missionary Nature of the Church*, 19.

14. Grammarians have noted the last clause of verse 3 could be translated as passive ("in you all ... shall be blessed"), reflexive "in you all ... shall bless themselves), or even in a middle voice ("in you all ... shall find blessing in you"). While there is practical truth to God's mission in each interpretation (i.e., Abraham is a conduit of blessing, Abraham is an example, Abraham is discovered by the nations), the passive is not only the traditional view but, according to Derek Kidner, the New Testament follows the LXX and views this text as passive (Acts 3:25; Gal 3:8). The LXX treats Genesis 22:18 and 26:4 as passive too. See Derek Kidner, *Genesis: An Introduction and Commentary* (Downers Grove, IL: InterVarsity Press, 1967), 114. Kenneth A. Matthews notes that the passive "probably suits the context of the passage best" (*Genesis 11:27–50:26* [Nashville: Broadman & Holman, 2005], 117). For an extensive treatment on the promises of God in this passage as well as a discussion of the grammar see Matthews, *Genesis 11:27–50:26*, 104–18.

15. Blauw, *The Missionary Nature of the Church*, 23.

purpose. This particularism was the means by which God would bring the nations to faith. Rather than Israel's election being a way to exclude the nations from God's blessings, it was the means of grace whereby the gentiles would come to know him. God's blessing of Israel defines the people in relationship to the other nations.[16] Through election the nations were included in the promise.[17] Israel would demonstrate her election through service, for as long as she remained faithful to the Lord, she was of the most value to the nations.[18]

God's interaction with Abraham, Isaac, and Jacob in relation to the Abrahamic covenant would be developed and reaffirmed in Genesis. God clarified Abraham's descendants would be as numerous as the stars:

> And he brought him outside and said, "Look toward heaven, and number the stars, if you are able to number them." Then he said to him, "So shall your offspring be." And he believed the LORD, and he counted it to him as righteousness. (Gen 15:5-6)

On this same evening, God formalized the covenant (Gen 15:9-17) and promised Abraham a great amount of land (Gen 15:18-21) which his descendants would obtain. God's presence, represented by the fire pot and flaming torch, passed between the sacrificed animals. God alone, rather than Abraham, assumed the covenant responsibilities and consequences if broken. Faithful to his word, his purpose in the world would be accomplished. Though the curse of sin rested on Abraham and his future descendants, God would uphold divine justice and fulfill the covenant. The writers of the New Testament note it is in Christ that God assumed the curses so that he would be glorified among the nations (cf. Rom 3:21-26; Gal 3:10-14).

Later, God declares he will make Abraham exceedingly fruitful, that kings will come from him, and his covenant with him is everlasting (Gen 17:4, 6-8).[19] This moment is marked with a change in nomenclature. No

---

16. Lucien Legrand, *Unity and Plurality: Mission in the Bible* (Maryknoll, NY: Orbis Books, 1990), 14.

17. Georg F. Vicedom, *The Mission of God: An Introduction to a Theology of Mission* (St. Louis: Concordia, 1965), 48.

18. See H. H. Rowley, *The Missionary Message of the Old Testament* (London: The Carey Kingsgate Press, 1944).

19. Paul references Gen 17:5 to draw attention to Abraham's faith and the need for everyone to follow in his steps to receive righteousness (Rom 4:17).

longer will God refer to him as Abram ("exalted father"), but will call him Abraham ("father of a multitude"), for God has made him "the father of a multitude of nations" (Gen 17:5). In a shocking turn of events, God tests Abraham by commanding him to sacrifice the son by which the promise would arrive. It is here the writer reveals that though God is the one who blesses, *relationship with him is paramount to things received from him*. Abraham's act is interrupted by God's messenger and Isaac is spared, but a ram is sacrificed in his place (Gen 22:13), a foreshadowing of the development of the subtheme of substitutionary atonement (Lev 1:4; 2 Cor 5:21). In view of his obedience, God's promise is restated to Abraham (Gen 22:15–18).[20] God would later reaffirm his covenant with Abraham by continuing the promises to Isaac (Gen 26:3–5). Jacob would also receive the reaffirmation and promises (Gen 28:13–15).

Toward the end of Genesis, the reader gains additional information regarding details of God's mission in the world. As Jacob blesses his sons prior to his death, he makes a statement regarding Judah that has been understood as a prophetic declaration of something great to come. While Judah will be praised and honored by his brothers and mighty against his enemies, the scepter and ruler's staff will not depart from him (Gen 49:8–10). These royal items that connote a powerful, eternal ruler to come are in line with God's promise to Abraham that "kings shall come from you" (Gen 17:6). Sadly, Israel casts aside the responsibility that comes with the privilege of Abraham's blessings.[21]

---

20. Peter draws from Genesis 22:18 to show that his contemporaries are initial beneficiaries of the Abrahamic covenant—that would result in the blessing of the nations (Acts 3:25–26).

21. Derek Kidner's synopsis of Israel's history is helpful in understanding the larger biblical narrative: "Blessing for the world was a vision fitfully seen at first (it disappears between the patriarchs and the kings, apart from a reminder of Israel's priestly role in Exod 19:5, 6). Later it reappeared in the psalms and prophets, and perhaps even at its faintest it always imparted some sense of mission to Israel; yet it never became a programme of concerted action until the ascension." *Genesis: An Introduction and Commentary* (Leicester, UK: Inter-Varsity Press, 1967), 114.

## BLESSING THE NATIONS
## THROUGH A PEOPLE: ISRAEL

The arrogance of the nations against God reveals the depravity and effects of sin (Gen 11:1–9). The need for Abraham is shown immediately following the Table of Nations (Gen 10–11). It was in the middle of the peoples of the earth that God was about to make room for a specific people related to his mission.[22] His approach to universal blessing continued in a particularistic direction through Abraham's descendants. The Hebrew people were chosen in Abraham to be God's treasured possession, and set "in praise and in fame and in honor high above all nations" (Deut 26:18–19). They were to represent God before all the peoples of the world. They were his chosen people.

One may ask, why this people? What was it that made Israel so special, so unique that the God who created everything from nothing would choose them? God chose them because of his love and covenantal faithfulness. He is gracious to whom he shows grace and merciful to whom he shows mercy (Exod 33:19). Deuteronomy emphasizes this truth but adds little to this reason:

> It was not because you were more in number than any other people that the LORD set his love on you and chose you, for you were the fewest of all peoples, but it is because the LORD loves you and is keeping the oath that he swore to your fathers. (Deut 7:7–8)[23]

Ezekiel notes Israel did not come from a righteous people. Rather, she came from the land of Canaan with an Amorite for a father and a Hittite for a mother (Ezek 16:3, 45). Despite her history, Israel was not to walk in the ways of her Canaanite ancestors but was to be "a people holy to the LORD" (Deut 26:19).

When God called Moses to deliver his people, he foretold pharaoh's recalcitrance (Exod 3:19) and the need for mighty acts leading to deliverance. However, there was another purpose for the signs and wonders. God was revealing himself to *Egypt that the world may know him.*

> For this time I will send all my plagues on you yourself, and on your servants and your people, so that you may know that there is none

---

22. Blauw, *The Missionary Nature of the Church*, 38.
23. See also Deuteronomy 4:37; 10:15; 14:1–2; 26:18–19.

like me in all the earth. For by now I could have put out my hand and stuck you and your people with pestilence and you would have been cut off from the earth. But for this purpose I have raised you up, to show you my power, so that my name may be proclaimed in all the earth. (Exod 9:14–16)[24]

While the plagues hardened pharaoh toward Israel and God, many people believed. On the night of the exodus, a mixed multitude fled Egypt with Israel (Exod 12:38). This fulfilled God's words to Moses that the Egyptians would come to know that he is the Lord (Exod 7:5).

Following the deliverance from Egypt, God brings Israel to Mount Sinai. Prior to giving the law, he reveals additional details regarding his mission.

They set out from Rephidim and came into the wilderness of Sinai, and they encamped in the wilderness. There Israel encamped before the mountain, while Moses went up to God. The Lord called to him out of the mountain, saying, "Thus you shall say to the house of Jacob, and tell the people of Israel: 'You yourselves have seen what I did to the Egyptians, and how I bore you on eagles' wings and brought you to myself. Now therefore, if you will indeed obey my voice and keep my covenant, you shall be my treasured possession among all peoples, for all the earth is mine; and you shall be to me a kingdom of priests and a holy nation.' These are the words that you shall speak to the people of Israel." (Exod 19:2–6)

Scholars agree on the significance of this passage expressing God's global plan even if they disagree on how that plan was to be executed. While Levi would become the official priestly tribe representing Israel before God at the tabernacle, all of Israel was to be holy priests in his kingdom.[25] The entire nation is sanctified and expected to reflect the glory of God on

---

24. Other "knowing" texts in Moses's interaction with Pharaoh include 8:22 and 9:30.

25. W. Ross Blackburn describes the nation as "a kingdom with a priestly function." *The God Who Makes Himself Known: The Missionary Heart of the Book of Exodus* (Downers Grove, IL: InterVarsity Press, 2012), 90.

earth.[26] It is from this relationship that purposeful acts come. As a kingdom of priests, they were to represent God before the nations and represent the nations before God.

God's people were relationally and categorically exceptional, with a unique purpose to fulfill on behalf of all other people.[27] The entire book of Exodus shows God's desire to make himself known through his elected people.[28]

God's love for the nations would later be noted in his clear instructions to Israel regarding the sojourners in their land. It was assumed that non-Hebrews would make their home alongside Israel. Whenever this occurred, Israel was to "treat the stranger who sojourns with you as the native among you." But the action did not stop here, for Israel was told "you shall love him as yourself, for you were strangers in the land of Egypt: I am the LORD your God" (Lev 19:34). The sojourner was allowed to keep the Passover (Exod 12:48). There would be no separate legal system for the stranger. Only one law was permitted for everyone (Exod 12:49). Israel was not allowed to take advantage of or oppress the people among her (Exod 22:21). Gentiles making offerings to the Lord were accepted like Jews (Num 15:14–16). Moses commanded Israel to read the law before all of the people every seven years. The gentiles were to be present for this public recital and receive blessings like the Jews:

> Assemble the people, men, women, and little ones, and the sojourner within your towns, that they may hear and learn to fear the LORD your God, and be careful to do all the words of this law, and that their children, who have not known it, may hear and learn to fear the LORD your God, as long as you live in the land that you are going over the Jordan to possess. (Deut 31:12–13)

The first four chapters of Deuteronomy retell Israel's history. It is in this section as Moses reminds the people of their past that he makes two

---

26. G. B. Caird writes, that Israel had a "special vocation of holiness" to display before God and the world (G. B. Caird, *A Commentary on the Revelation of St. John the Divine* [New York: Harper & Row, 1966], 17).

27. Blauw, *The Missionary Nature of the Church*, 28.

28. Blackburn, *The God Who Makes Himself Known*, 20.

important points related to God's mission. First, God is sovereign over all nations. And second, Israel's reception of the promised land was not an unusual act of God's grace toward a nation.

While Israel traveled from Egypt to the promised land, she was not to contend with Edom. She was not to harass Moab or Ammon. None of the land of these peoples would be given to Israel. Why? Because God had "given Mount Seir to Esau as a possession" (Deut 2:5), "Ar to the people of Lot for a possession" (Deut 2:9), and Ammon's land to its people (Deut 2:19). Moses's words were to humble Israel while recognizing God had shed his grace on others too; God gave land to other nations, but Israel was unique in its particular covenant relationship to God.[29] The words that followed in Deuteronomy were holy and called for a sober heart. Israel was just like the nations, except for her God.

While Israel was to find life through her relationship to God and obedience to his statutes and rules (Deut 4:1), her obedience was a witness to the nations. Israel was to keep and do the statutes, "for that will be your wisdom and your understanding in the sight of the peoples, who, when they hear all these statutes, will say, 'Surely this great nation is a wise and understanding people'" (Deut 4:6). The nations' observations would cause them to ask with excitement, "What great nation is there that has a god so near to it as the LORD" (Deut 4:7)?

The land that had been promised to Abraham four centuries prior was to be the epicenter of God's mission in the world. The conquest and reception of the land was a significant event on his timetable. Though he brought them to Canaan's border, Israel chose to walk away from God. The majority report from the twelve spies won the hearts of the people. Cowering in fear, they wept and believed God was taking them into the promised land to be killed by the sword (Num 14:3). Israel decided it would be better to return to Egyptian slavery and desired a leader to lead them back to their chains (Num 14:4). In the midst of such chaos, God pardons the people of their rebellion and makes a fascinating claim about his mission in the judgment that is to come. He informs Moses the rebellious adults will not see the promised land and guarantees their death based on his constant existence and *inevitable mission*: "But truly, as I live, and as all the earth

---

29. Christopher Wright, *Deuteronomy* (Peabody, MA: Hendrickson, 1996), 36.

shall be filled with the glory of the LORD, none of the men who have seen my glory and my signs that I did in Egypt and in the wilderness. ... shall see the land that I swore to their fathers" (Num 14:21–23).

After the forty years of wandering, the new generation is reminded of the covenant blessings. If they remain faithful and keep all of God's commandments, they will be set high above all nations (Deut 28:1). The Sinai language of a specific, holy people is repeated:

> The LORD will establish you as a people holy to himself, as he has sworn to you, if you keep the commandments of the LORD your God and walk in his ways. And all the peoples of the earth shall see that you are called by the name of the LORD and they shall be afraid of you." (Deut 28:9–10)

## BLESSING THE NATIONS THROUGH A PRESENCE: TABERNACLE

God's mission in the world involves an intimate relationship with those made in his image. This relationship cannot be separated from obedience to his word. God has always been *with* his creation. When Adam heard God in the garden, he was afraid and hid because of the shame from the severed relationship (Gen 3:8–10). Abraham understood that relationship with God superseded the value of receiving things from God. Moses also recognized the intimacy of relationship and desired to see God's glory (Exod 33:16, 18). He understood the significance of the divine presence, without which he did not want to enter into the promised land. God's presence with his people would make them distinct and set them apart "from every other people on the face of the earth" (Exod 33:16). Moses knew fellowship with God could be broken and would need restoration. Without this relationship, Israel could not participate in God's mission in the world. But Israel was a sinful people. How could the fellowship remain? How was she to survive, either in the wilderness or promised land, with a holy and fiery God dwelling in her presence? The answer would come in the form of the tabernacle and cultic practices. The tabernacle and covenantal faithfulness would be a means toward a restored fellowship and testimony to the nations.

The tabernacle was significant to Israel's religious practices and identity as the people of God. Its physical design contained echoes of Eden and represented all of creation.[30] This portable tent with its curtains and contents represented God's presence among his people (Exod 25:8, 22; 30:6, 36). The transcendent God who created everything and called a particular people to himself revealed his immanent nature by placing himself in the camp. The tabernacle would serve as a visual reminder that God has not only blessed Israel above all peoples as a kingdom of priests and holy nation (Exod 19:5-6), but that her intimacy with him was vital to her blessings and global purpose.[31] Israel's witness to the world was to have a centripetal effect on the nations. Her relationship with God would result in blessings that would capture the attention of others. Israel would become a living challenge, extended to all that they may come and see that the Lord is good.

The tabernacle represented a message of hope through judgment. The sacrificial system to be conducted there was a perennial reminder to Israel and the world that relationship with God and his blessings were related to the evil of sin and substitutionary atonement. Life in his kingdom had to be lived according to his desires. The nations of the world could not approach him on their terms. His ethic demanded a specificity as articulated in his Torah given to Israel. The love of Israel's God, reflected in his dwelling among them (cf. John 1:14), was manifested both toward the children of Abraham and the nations. The tabernacle served to remind Israel of her responsibility to communicate the message that if the nations wanted to know and experience the blessings of their Creator, then they should look to Israel and join her before the tabernacle.

## CONCLUSION

The Pentateuch concludes with Israel about to receive land promised to Abraham. However, a distinct irony is found in the latter sections. Though Israel was to carry out God's purpose in the world, she would fail at this task (Deut 32). Her sinful nature would render impossible the assignment

---

30. On the use of this language and an extensive treatment of correspondences between the tabernacle to the created order see Blackburn, *The God Who Makes Himself Known*, 135–42 and Beale, *The Temple and the Church's Mission*, 60–63, 66–80.

31. Blackburn writes, "If the Lord was sought through obedience to his commands, and obedience to his commands was the means by which Israel fulfilled her intended missionary function among the nations (19:4-6), then Israel's seeking the Lord cannot be separated from her missionary function. As Israel sought the Lord, obeying his law, she fulfilled her missionary function." *The God Who Makes Himself Known*, 134.

before her. Someone even greater than Abraham, Moses, or the nation would be required to fulfill God's desires. Commenting on this matter, N. T. Wright notes:

> The repeated biblical promises of divine blessing and new creation for the world were to be attained by the obedience of Israel. But, faced with Israel's disobedience, the mission of God could only be accomplished through the single faithful Israelite, the Messiah, coming to the place of rebellion, the place where the world's wickedness would reach its height and the divine love would reach its depth.[32]

Even the presence of the tabernacle was insufficient to maintain Israel's faithfulness to God. Though this tent would be replaced with Solomon's temple, physical holy structures are unable to overcome the effects of sin. Though they represent relationship with the Creator, they are distinct from him and no substitute for him. The intimacy Adam and Eve had with God in the garden had been lost. Though the presence of the tabernacle was a message of judgment, it was also a message of hope. The experience of Eden was gone, but God still loved his people and placed himself among them.

Centuries later, John draws heavily from the language of Torah in the prologue to his Gospel to reveal a greater development in God's mission. *In the beginning* was God. Taking on flesh, he *tabernacled* among his people (John 1:1; 14). Seeing the new heaven and new earth, the apostle heard a voice that proclaimed, "Behold, the dwelling place of God is with man. He will dwell with them, and they will be his people, and God himself will be with them as their God" (Rev 21:3). Just as the tabernacle in the Old Testament was a physical representation of God with his people in fellowship and mission, the New Testament language builds upon the Old Testament theology and carries it to fulfillment and greater understanding of the promises found in the Noahic, Abrahamic, and Mosaic covenants. But before we can get to the New Testament, we must consider the subthemes that support God's mission found in the Prophets and Writings.

---

32. Wright, "The Bible and Christian Mission," 391.

## REFLECTION QUESTIONS

1. Do you think God's mission is still to fill the earth with his image-bearers that glorify himself? Why?

2. What is a covenant?

3. If God is omnipresent, then why did he limit himself to the tabernacle and just Israel?

## CHAPTER 4

# Mission in the Prophets

THE HEBREW SCRIPTURES are organized into three sections: Torah, Prophets, and Writings. Beginning with creation and Adam and concluding with the rebuilding of the temple in Jerusalem, this organization provides the text with a discernable structure that points to God's relationship and blessing to sinful people.[1] Though the relationship begins with intimacy but follows with separation, the storyline concludes with a focus on David's dynasty and a new temple that points to a future restoration and greater glory to come.[2]

Chapters 4 and 5 follow the organization of the Hebrew Scriptures while addressing mission in the Prophets and Writings. A proper understanding of God's mission may be obtained through the Old Testament structure. However, I have found the Hebrew Scriptures' organization provides a concise and helpful approach to understanding Israel's history and God's message of hope through judgment.

The Prophets are organized into the Former (Joshua, Judges, Samuel, and Kings) and Latter (Isaiah, Jeremiah, Ezekiel, the Twelve) Prophets. This series

---

1. The Hebrew Scriptures concludes with Chronicles (i.e., 1–2 Chronicles) which includes the people of Israel returning to the land to rebuild the temple. Though the Old Testament concludes with Malachi, pointing to a forthcoming Elijah and day of the Lord, the Hebrew Scriptures' structure also reflects an eschatological reality that being a new temple in which the Messiah would visit as the prophets foresaw. The belief that the structure of the Hebrew Scriptures signifies completion and focuses on ethics while the Old Testament concludes with an anticipation of fulfillment and focuses on eschatological matters is reductionistic and an unnecessary dichotomy. See Stephen G. Dempster, *Dominion and Dynasty: A Theology of the Hebrew Bible* (Downers Grove, IL: InterVarsity Press, 2003), 40.

2. Dempster, *Dominion and Dynasty*, 45–51.

of writings not only addresses Israel's history but offers much perspective on the mission of God. The Former Prophets describe general historical events and the theological matters related to Israel during those times. They cover the period from Israel's entrance into Canaan until the Babylonian invasion and exile. The Latter Prophets offer specific and extensive treatment related to Israel's major historical events.[3] Prophecy interprets history and explains why Israel lost her great blessings and entered into exile. The work of the prophets provides warnings to avoid past mistakes but points to Israel's best days found in the future. Hope is found through judgment. It is especially noteworthy that the Prophets' statements regarding Israel's future blessings are related to the nations' future blessings.[4]

God's mission is revealed throughout the Prophets. While they address the themes of sin, judgment, and restoration, these issues are connected to God's work in and through His people to be a blessing to the nations. The Prophets call Israel to covenantal faithfulness. Israel's faith and obedience results in both blessing to Israel and awe among the nations. But before examining the Prophets, it is important to understand how the Hebrew Scriptures describe the methods by which the gentiles come to serve the God of Israel.

## MOVEMENT OF THE GENTILES: INCORPORATION AND INGATHERING

There are two methods of gentile conversion: *historical incorporation* and *eschatological ingathering*.[5] Throughout Israel's history, provision was made for gentiles submitting themselves to the God of Israel. While Israel did not practice an aggressive missionary religion, the Hebrew Scriptures show special concern for gentile "sojourners" in Israel. [6] In many cases, these gentiles were assimilated into the people of Israel over time, generally

---

3. Paul R. House and Eric Mitchell, *Old Testament Survey,* 2nd ed. (Nashville: B&H Academic, 2007), 89. Dempster argues the Latter Prophets, along with a portion of the Writings, fall in the middle of the Hebrew Scriptures. They serve to create a pause in the biblical storyline and offer commentary on the exile and vision of the future (Dempster, *Dominion and Dynasty*, 50).

4. Mitchell, *Old Testament Survey,*, 177–78.

5. Charles H. H. Scobie makes this argument. See his "Israel and the Nations: An Essay in Biblical Theology." *Tyndale Bulletin* 43, no. 2 (1992): 283–305.

6. Scobie, "Israel and the Nations," 286–87.

through a centripetal means. Rahab and Ruth are two examples of this method—historical incorporation. These women decided to unite with Israel after learning about God and his work through his people.

The Hebrew Scriptures also speak of a gathering of the nations before the day of the Lord—or eschatological ingathering. Much of what we know about this eschatological method in the Old Testament is found in the Prophets, and primarily described as occurring through a centripetal means. They announce a future day that would involve the nations streaming to Jerusalem and uniting with the people of God. This prediction of a gathering of the nations into Israel during the last days helps us understand the New Testament's mission to the gentiles.[7] Therefore, more will be said about the ingathering and the church in subsequent chapters. For now, we shall note how the Prophets address both of these methods.

## FORMER PROPHETS

### BLESSING THE NATIONS THROUGH A PLACE: PROMISED LAND

Following the death of Moses, Joshua leads Israel into the promised land (Josh 1:1–3). The new generation did not rebel as their predecessors. The sins of the Amorites had reached their full measure (Gen 15:16), and the long-suffering of God had expired. Israel's hope for rest would come, but through judgment on the nations. Israel was to serve as a sword in the hand of God by conquering and taking the Canaanites' land. God told Israel whenever she conquered the land she was not to believe that victory was determined by her righteousness. In fact, it is clear Israel's righteousness did not exceed the righteousness of the Egyptians or Canaanites. Rather, it was because of the nations' wickedness that they were being driven out, as well as to confirm the promise to the patriarchs (Deut 9: 4–5). The time of judgment had arrived. Israel would soon receive what God had promised and would serve as a light to the nations. God had called Israel, his son,

---

7. Scobie, "Israel and the Nations," 283.

from Egypt (Exod 4:22–23; Hos 11:1; cf. Matt 2:15) and was about to place the people in a highly strategic location for his mission.[8]

The book of Joshua provides a glimpse into the process by which gentiles would come to unite with God's people. Early in the book, Rahab and her family are spared destruction with the fall of Jericho (Josh 6:25). Her declaration of the fear of the Lord was made clear to the spies:

> For we have heard how the LORD dried up the water of the Red Sea before you when you came out of Egypt, and what you did to the two kings of the Amorites who were beyond the Jordan, to Sihon and Og, whom you devoted to destruction ... for the LORD your God, he is God in the heavens above and on the earth beneath. (Josh 2:10, 11)

When Israel established a memorial after they crossed the Jordan, Joshua explained part of the reason for God's mighty acts on behalf of his people:

> For the LORD your God dried up the waters of the Jordan for you until you passed over, as the LORD your God did to the Red Sea, which he dried up for us until we passed over, so that all the peoples of the earth may know that the hand of the LORD is mighty, that you may fear the LORD your God forever. (Josh 4:23–24)

Israel was to fear the Lord, but such divine acts also served as a witness to the gentiles. Just as Rahab noted the reputation of God and Israel had preceded their arrival into the promised land, other nations would hear and recognize that Israel's God is different and powerful. Rahab's entrance into the people of God by faith was brought about through a message of judgment with hope. Though Jericho would be destroyed, Rahab and her household would be spared by following the spies' instructions. Her historical incorporation into God's people was considered noteworthy among the New Testament writers (Matt 1:5; Heb 11:31; Jas 2:25).

---

8. Peter J. Gentry and Stephen J. Wellum comment on the nation's location in the Fertile Crescent: "Since Israel is located geographically on the one and only communications link between the great superpowers of the ancient world, in this position she will show the nations how to have a right relationship to God, how to treat each other in a truly human way, and how to be faithful stewards of the earth's resources." *Kingdom through Covenant*, 399.

## BLESSING THE NATIONS THROUGH
## A PERSON: A KING FOR ALL

The beginning of Israel's monarchy marked a significant transition in the history of God's people. Israel would no longer be a loosely confederated network of twelve tribes. The period of the judges transitioned to the time of the prophets. Israel's political, economic, and religious systems would become more defined under a unified government. Torah allowed for the establishment of a monarchy, provided the people and king followed God's guidelines (Deut 17:14-20). Though Israel's initial request for a ruler occurred with wrong motives (1 Sam 8), God granted her petition. Saul became the nation's first king, rebelled against God, and was rejected by God (1 Sam 9-10; 15). David was chosen to become Saul's successor (1 Sam 16) and was the recipient of a covenant that marked a significant development in the biblical storyline and God's mission.[9]

After David is told he will not be permitted to build the temple, God reveals to him what has been called the Davidic covenant (2 Sam 7:1-17) with the following promises to David regarding Israel's future and his royal descendant:

- "I will make for you a great name" (2 Sam 7:9).

- "I will appoint a place for my people Israel … so they may dwell in their own place and be disturbed no more" (2 Sam 7:10).

- "I will give you rest from all your enemies" (2 Sam 7:11).

- "I will raise up your offspring after you (2 Sam 7:12).

- "I will establish … his kingdom forever" (2 Sam 7:13).

- "I will be to him a father, and he shall be to me a son" (2 Sam 7:14).

- "When he commits iniquity, I will discipline him" (2 Sam 7:14).

---

9. Long before the Davidic covenant was established, David desired God's glory to be among the nations. On the day of battle with the Philistine, David exclaimed the giant would be defeated and "all the earth may know that there is a God in Israel, and that all this assembly may know that the LORD saves not with sword and spear" (1 Sam 17:46-47). In an amazing turn, Zechariah would later foretell of a day when the Philistines would be united with YHWH and his people (Zech 9:7).

- "My steadfast love will not from depart him" (2 Sam 7:15).

- "Your house and your kingdom shall be made sure forever before me. Your throne shall be established forever" (2 Sam 7:16).

God's words echo aspects of the Abrahamic covenant. Portions of the Davidic covenant were designed to fulfill that which was promised to Abraham. God's plan involves a Davidic king who would be for all nations. After he receives God's words, he declares, "this is instruction for mankind" (2 Sam 7:19), not just Israel. The covenant is to be fulfilled by both a faithful father (i.e., YHWH) and a faithful son (i.e., king).[10] Therefore, a covenant that establishes the Davidic king as God's son is the means of "bringing Yahweh's Torah to all the nations."[11] Later passages such as Psalm 72:17 and Isaiah 55 point to a future king whose love and acts will bring blessing to the peoples as he delivers Torah to them.[12] Taken together, it is very likely David understood the universal significance of this covenant, though not the details revealed to the first century disciples. While the children of Abraham received many blessings from God and became a great nation (Gen 12:2), all the families of the earth were to be blessed (Gen 12:3). The king was to live and lead Israel according to Torah (Deut 17:18–20). In doing so, the mission of God would extend through them to the nations. All would be blessed who take refuge in the Lord's Son, of the Davidic dynasty (Psalm 2:12).

## BLESSING THE NATIONS THROUGH A PRESENCE: TEMPLE

Though David had a noble vision of building a permanent structure for the ark of God, he was not allowed to accomplish this task (1 Kgs 5:3). Rather, God promised he would build David an eternal kingdom (2 Sam 7:11). Solomon, however, would receive the blessing of building God's temple (2 Sam 7:13).[13]

---

10. While Israel is referred to as God's son (Exod 4:22–23; Hos 11:1), here the king receives this title as well (cf. Matt 2:15).

11. Gentry and Wellum, *Kingdom through Covenant*, 399.

12. Gentry and Wellum, *Kingdom through Covenant*, 424.

13. The Chronicler attributes God's denial to David because he was a man of war. Solomon, a man of rest, receives the building permit (1 Chr 22:8–10).

The reign of Solomon marked the zenith of Israel's wealth, peace, prosperity, and influence. The writer of Kings notes:

Judah and Israel were as many as the sand by the sea. They ate and drank and were happy. Solomon ruled over all the kingdoms from the Euphrates to the land of the Philistines and to the border of Egypt. They brought tribute and served Solomon all the days of his life. (1 Kgs 4:20–21)

The manifestation of God's mission is developed in this passage. The children of Abraham became innumerable, received a vast amount of promised land, and experienced rest and delight under the Davidic dynasty. The nations knew the relationship of Israel with her God. Such global knowledge and awe would soon increase with another significant milestone in the mission: the construction of the temple.

Solomon began construction in the fourth year of his reign, which was 480 years after the exodus (1 Kgs 6:1). With Israel settled in the land and "rest on every side" (1 Kgs 5:4), the mobile structure of the tabernacle would be replaced with a building. A temple to God would serve as the new permanent location for the ark and center of Israel's religious system.

Solomon's prayer of dedication for the temple provides important insight into God's mission as noted in the Former Prophets:

Likewise, when a foreigner, who is not of your people Israel, comes from a far country for your name's sake (for they shall hear of your great name and your mighty hand, and of your outstretched arm), when he comes and prays toward this house, hear in heaven your dwelling place and do according to all for which the foreigner calls to you ... as do your people Israel, and that they may know that this house that I have built is called by your name (1 Kgs 8:41–43).

Solomon foresees that God's reputation through Israel will continue to spread among the nations. The construction of this edifice will make the news. The peoples will hear the stories of old as well as God's present relationship with his people. This testimony will be used by God to draw the nations to Jerusalem for prayer. Anyone who comes will not be cast away. Solomon then makes a remarkable request on behalf of the gentiles. He asks God to grant to the foreigner all of his or her petitions! The stories of the history of Israel's God, his blessings observed in Jerusalem, and answered prayers were a powerful triad of divine witness to the one true God. Solomon recognizes this testimony and concludes his prayer with the expectation "that all the peoples of the earth may know that the LORD is God; there is no other" (1 Kgs 8:60).

The writer then illustrates Solomon's hope. After the completion of the temple, the Queen of Sheba arrives in Jerusalem to visit the king. She heard of his fame "concerning the name of the LORD" (1 Kgs 10:1). Witnessing the blessings of God, she declared to Solomon, "Blessed be the LORD your God, who has delighted in you and set you on the throne of Israel! Because the LORD loved Israel forever, he has made you king, that you may execute justice and righteousness" (1 Kgs 10:9). The arrival of the queen foreshadows the movement of the nations to Jerusalem, a matter developed in the Latter Prophets. The king's wealth continues to increase so that "Solomon excelled all the kings of the earth in riches and in wisdom" (1 Kgs 10:23). What God did in and through Israel served as a magnet drawing the nations to Jerusalem for "the whole earth sought the presence of Solomon to hear his wisdom, which God had put into his mind" (1 Kgs 10:24).

## DIVIDED KINGDOM AND EXILE

David's sin resulted in both his downfall and the division within his household (2 Sam 12:10–12). Though Solomon achieved many outstanding accomplishments, several of his actions brought God's great displeasure and resulted in the division of the nation:

> And the LORD was angry with Solomon, because his heart had turned away from the LORD, the God of Israel, who had appeared to him twice and had commanded him concerning this thing, that he should not go after other gods. But he did not keep what the LORD commanded. Therefore the LORD said to Solomon, "Since this has been your practice and you have not kept my covenant and my statutes that I have commanded you, I will surely tear the kingdom from you and will give it to your servant. Yet for the sake of David your father I will not do it in your days, but I will tear it out of the hand of your son. However, I will not tear away all the kingdom, but I will

give one tribe to your son, for the sake of David my servant and for the sake of Jerusalem that I have chosen." (1 Kgs 11:9–13)

Following Solomon's death, the nation divided with ten tribes comprising the northern territory and two tribes the southern territory.[14] King Jeroboam established Shechem as his home and developed a religious system for the north (1 Kgs 12:25–33). Samaria was established as the capital in the north (1 Kgs 16:24), while Jerusalem remained the capital of the south. The nation would be divided for over 300 years until the Babylonian exile. The book of Kings has little good to say about the actions of any of the monarchs. Israel failed to manifest what it meant to be a holy nation and royal priesthood before God and the nations. She gave up the great responsibilities that came with her election, consumed God's blessings for selfish gain through idolatrous acts, and became like the nations around her.

The northern kingdom experienced the Assyrian invasion and destruction of their territory in 722 BC (2 Kgs 17:6). Though the South avoided the Assyrian destruction, her sins caught up with her. In 587 BC, Babylon invaded her territory, destroyed the temple and Jerusalem, and deported the people (2 Kgs 25:1–21). Why did such devastation occur? Were the gods of Babylon greater than YHWH? Did YHWH give up on his people? Was God's mission finished? Both the Former and Latter Prophets answer these questions.

With the people exiled from the land and the throne and temple destroyed, it appeared as if God's promises to Abraham, Israel, and David had come to an end. Torah promised these horrible results for sin (Deut 4:27–29; 28:25–37). God had explained to Solomon that rebellion would result in such destruction and exile (1 Kgs 9:6–9). By 587 BC, the people who were to extend blessing to the nations became a dreaded "proverb and a byword" (1 Kgs 9:7). Israel became known for abandoning the God who had blessed her.

---

14. The north embraced the name "Israel" and the south "Judah."

## LATTER PROPHETS

Isaiah, Jeremiah, Ezekiel, and the Twelve write extensively regarding what they observed during their days and foresaw in both the near and distant future.[15] The Latter Prophets represent a great deal of diversity in the Old Testament. Numerous personalities, themes (i.e., sin, judgment, and restoration), and writing styles are contained in these books. At least four periods of time are addressed by different authors (i.e., fall of Samaria by Assyria, fall of Jerusalem by Babylon, return from Babylonian exile, and the days of Ezra and Nehemiah). This section attempts to address the following matters and their relation to the mission of God: judgment on Israel, Israel's return to the land, messianic servant, new covenant, outpouring of the Spirit, gentile ingathering, day of the Lord, and restoration.

## BLESSING THE NATIONS THROUGH JUDGMENT: ISRAEL IN DIASPORA

The restoration and healing of the nations was dependent on Israel's existence and reception of God's blessings. Judgment on Israel affected the entire world. Torah described the consequences of breaking the covenant (Lev 18:24-28; 26:14-33; Deut 4:25-28; 28:15-68; 29:24-28). Proclaiming the word of the Lord, Jeremiah noted, "my people have committed two evils: they have forsaken me, the fountain of living waters, and hewed out cisterns for themselves, broken cisterns that can hold no water" (Jer 2:13). Just as God remained faithful to his word regarding his blessings on Israel, he was faithful when Israel fell short of his standard. God's people, though elect, are still held accountable.[16] God had called his people to himself and expected their faithfulness. Israel was to love the Lord with all of her heart, soul, and might (Deut 6:5). Leviticus described the actions she was to take whenever she sinned. As the nation and her leaders transitioned away from covenantal faithfulness, the promises of Deuteronomy came to pass. Israel would lose the land of promise.

---

15. A single work in the Tanakh, the Twelve consists of what is normally called the Minor Prophets (i.e., Hosea, Joel, Amos, Obadiah, Jonah, Micah, Nahum, Habakkuk, Zephaniah, Haggai, Zechariah, and Malachi).

16. James Chukwuma Okoye, *Israel and the Nations: A Mission Theology of the Old Testament* (Maryknoll, NY: Orbis Books, 2006), 70.

Before this act of judgment, God graciously sent prophets to his people. They continued to call attention to the sound of sabers rattling on the distant horizon. If Israel did not repent, she would soon experience the opposition of the nations. Of all the people in the world, Israel should have known better. She heard God's voice, saw his power, and received his standard. With great blessing came great responsibility. She had been a sword of judgment in the hand of the Lord toward the Canaanites, but now her enemies would serve the same purpose against her. She was known by the Lord and would be punished for her iniquities (Amos 3:2).

Hosea called Israel to recognize her sin and repent of her unfaithfulness (Hos 4:1; 5:1). Amos brought attention to the oppression to come:

> "For behold, I will raise up against you a nation, O house of Israel," declares the LORD, the God of hosts; "and they shall oppress you from Lebo-hamath to the Brook of the Arabah." (Amos 6:14)

Isaiah warned "the wealth of Damascus and the spoil of Samaria will be carried away before the king of Assyria" (Isa 8:4). Habakkuk was told God was going to deal with the violence and injustice among Israel by raising up the Chaldeans who would bring greater violence and injustice to the land (Hab 1:1–11).

The judgment that came reveals that God is no respecter of persons. He can give blessings and take them away. The nations that should have been amazed at the relationship between Israel and God scoffed and mocked at the descendants of Abraham (2 Kgs 18:19–25). The people who were to be a servant of the Lord (Isa 44:1) became a laughingstock. Israel had failed to be part of the mission to transform the nations, and now the nations would transform Israel.

The prophets reveal that Israel and her kings were unable to be the faithful son of the Davidic covenant to bring Torah to the nations. They understood this matter and foresaw a future servant of the Lord (a Davidic descendant) who would be able to accomplish God's mission in the world.

During the suffering and loss, Jeremiah's message included an element of hope. While Israel would remain in captivity for seventy years, the Lord offered encouragement:

Thus says the LORD of hosts, the God of Israel, to all the exiles whom I have sent into exile from Jerusalem to Babylon: Build houses and live in them; plant gardens and eat their produce. Take wives and have sons and daughters; take wives for your sons, and give your daughters in marriage, that they may bear sons and daughters; multiply there, and do not decrease. But seek the welfare of the city where I have sent you into exile, and pray to the LORD on its behalf, for in its welfare you will find your welfare. (Jer 29:4–7)

The prophet's statement was simply if Israel desired ease in captivity, then she should do all within her power to make certain the city prospered. However, given God's mission to the nations would not be thwarted, could there be another meaning in this passage? Could this reflect divine irony? Rebellious Israel did not walk uprightly before the Lord and failed to display her calling as a holy nation. Since the nations were not attracted to her, could it be that God would send Israel to the nations, via Babylon (and Assyria)? God is not finished with them. He notes the exiles, even in captivity, had a task to accomplish.[17]

## BLESSING THE NATIONS THROUGH RESTORATION: RETURN AND RECONSTRUCTION

When Babylon was besieging Jerusalem, the Lord sent Jeremiah a puzzling message: purchase a piece of family property. Confused, the prophet sought the Lord's counsel and was told this purchase foreshadowed the reality that "houses and fields and vineyards shall again be bought in this land" (Jer 32:15). God promised that following the exile:

I will gather them from all the countries to which I drove them in my anger and my wrath and in great indignation. I will bring them back to this place, and I will make them dwell in safety. And they shall be my people, and I will be their God. I will give them one heart

---

17. Christopher J. H. Wright recognizes an allusion to the Abrahamic covenant when the prophet calls Israel to multiply in exile. God is not finished with them: "So they were not only to be the *beneficiaries* of God's promise to Abraham (in that they would not die out but increase), they were also to be the *agents* of God's promise to Abraham that through his descendants the nations would be blessed. The promise had said "all nations" –enemy nations not excluded. So let Israel assume the Abrahamic position in Babylon." *The Mission of God: Unlocking the Bible's Grand Narrative* (Downers Grove, IL: IVP Academic, 2006), 100.

and one way, that they may fear me forever, for their own good and the good of their children after them. I will make with them an everlasting covenant, that I will not turn away from doing good to them. And I will put the fear of me in their hearts, that they may not turn from me. (Jer 32:37-40)

How long would the exile last? When would Israel be permitted to return to the land? The Lord informs Jeremiah captivity would last seventy years. After this time, the Lord says, "I will visit you, and I will fulfill to you my promise and bring you back to this place. For I know the plans I have for you, declares the LORD, plans for welfare and not for evil, to give you a future and a hope" (Jer 29:10-11).

Ezekiel explained why God would move among his people, return them to the land, and make them prosperous. Was it because Israel was a needy people? Hardly. Was God showing compassion toward them because he felt pity? Though God loved them, such was not Ezekiel's answer. Rather, his holiness was on display:

> Therefore say to the house of Israel, Thus says the LORD God: It is not for your sake, O house of Israel, that I am about to act, but for the sake of my holy name, which you have profaned among the nations to which you came. And I will vindicate the holiness of my great name, which has been profaned among the nations, and which you have profaned among them. And the nations will know that I am the LORD, declares the LORD God, when through you I vindicate my holiness before their eyes. ... It is not for your sake that I will act, declares the LORD God; let that be known to you. (Ezek 36:22-23, 32)

Jeremiah's message to Israel was one of hope but filled with judgment related to her captors. He foretold the Lord would use the Medes and Persians to defeat Babylon (Jer 51:11). Israel would return to her homeland (Jer 25:11-14; 29:10-14), for God would bring defeat to the Babylonians. Isaiah prophesied Cyrus would be God's anointed to carry out his mission in the world (Isa 44:28-45:7).[18] In 539 BC, the Persians, led by Cyrus the Great, defeated Babylon. Cyrus made a decree that former Babylonian captives

---

18. For a helpful discussion of Isaiah's prediction of Cyrus see J. Alec Motyer, *Isaiah: An Introduction and Commentary* (Downers Grove, IL: InterVarsity Press, 1999), 318-346.

could return to their homelands. Ezra-Nehemiah and the Chronicler reminded their audiences of this prophecy (2 Chr 36:22–23; Ezra 1:1–4; cf. Prov 21:1). Ezekiel prophesied a day would arrive when Israel would return, and the nations would know that YHWH is "the LORD who sanctifies Israel" after he reestablishes his "sanctuary" among the people (Ezek 37:28). Such messages provided Israel hope, yet the reality contained echoes of judgment. Israel would return and enjoy many freedoms, but would remain in bondage to the Persians and their successors. The full restoration foretold by the prophets did not arrive with Cyrus's degree, but their return to the land was a necessary development before the arrival of Messiah.

Following the Babylonian captivity, Haggai corrects the people who desire to delay the reconstruction of the temple (Hag 1:2–11). God has withheld blessings because the people have forgotten the temple. The second temple, constructed by Zerubbabel, was smaller than Solomon's temple. This restoration foreshadowed a future greater grandeur. The Messiah would eventually come to the temple. However, his visit would result in a violent rebuke of the money changers for taking the place of *prayer for the nations* and transforming it into a den of thieves (Matt 21:13; Luke 19:46). Despite this future event recorded in the Gospels, Haggai noted the Lord would bring about a greater glory with this temple that involved the nations of the world:

> My Spirit remains in your midst. Fear not. For thus says the LORD of hosts: Yet once more, in a little while, I will shake the heavens and the earth and the sea and the dry land. And I will shake all nations, so that the treasures of all nations shall come in, and I will fill this house with glory, says the LORD of hosts. The silver is mine, and the gold is mind, declares the LORD of hosts. The latter glory of this house shall be greater than the former, says the LORD of hosts. And in this place I will give peace, declares the LORD of hosts. (Hag 2:4–9)[19]

---

19. The Lord of the second temple would arrive in the first century (John 2:13–22) with a glory that exceed anything observed in Solomon's temple.

Prior to the destruction of Jerusalem, Ezekiel declared God's glory departed the temple (Ezek 10–11), but an amazing temple was to come (Ezek 40–47:12). Haggai comforts the people. God would very soon bring the nations to Jerusalem, the place of peace; the temple would be the focal point of God's salvific interaction with the world.[20] Israel had been a "byword of cursing among the nations," but the Lord, true to his word, promised to save her that she shall be a blessing (Zech 8:13).

## BLESSING THE NATIONS THROUGH A PERSON: THE SERVANT

Though Cyrus may have allowed Israel to return home, she was still under Persian rule. The Davidic kingdom had not been reestablished. In this situation, Isaiah notes a day will come when peace, freedom, and the Lord's salvation will arrive through a future servant. This king will bring redemption, judgment, and restoration of all things (Isa 65:17–25). The Prophets contain passages that often had immediate, or near-future fulfillments, as well as distant fulfillments. Many of these latter prophecies are labeled "messianic" as they can be interpreted as an anointed individual who provides service and leadership from YHWH.

Isaiah's Servant Songs cover several chapters (42:1–4; 49:1–6; 50:4–9; 52:13–53:12) and describes one filled with the Spirit of God who will bring justice to the nations (42:1).[21] His service will turn Israel back to God (49:5). But his role is not exclusively for Israel. YHWH states his servant will be "a light for the nations, that my salvation may reach to the ends of the earth" (Isa 49:6).[22] The servant would achieve what Israel failed to accomplish before the peoples of the world. He would bear witness to God and Torah.

---

20. Joyce G. Baldwin, *Haggai, Zechariah and Malachi: An Introduction and Commentary* (Downers Grove, IL: InterVarsity Press, 1972), 52.

21. Rowley notes the Servant has a fluid identification in Isaiah. He writes, "The Servant is Israel, with a mission to the world; the Servant is also the spiritual Israel within Israel, with a mission to the rest of Israel as well as to the world; and … the Servant is also an individual in whom the mission reaches its climax, and whose work becomes the inspiration of the mission and the power wherein it can be achieved." Rowley, *The Missionary Message of the Old Testament*, 58.

22. Rowley comments that within the Servant Songs, "Nowhere in the Old Testament do we find the world vison more clearly expressed; nowhere do we find so clear a call to active

Unlike anything expected of Israel, the servant's service is taken to a supernatural level of relationship and blessing through judgment. In a cleansing and atoning fashion (Isa 52:15; cf. Exod 29:21; Lev 8:11; 14:7; 16:14–16), the servant will purify the nations. His ministry will come with great suffering (52:14; 53:3–5).[23] In a shocking set of words, the prophet notes the peace he brings will come through bearing the sin of others (Isa 53:5–9, 12). Though innocent, he will serve as a substitute, suffer, and die at the hands of YHWH (53:9–10), but he will somehow return to the land of the living (Isa 53:10–11). The servant will be "high and lifted up, and shall be exalted" (52:13).

Jeremiah writes a time is coming when the Lord "will raise up for David a righteous Branch, and he shall reign as king and deal wisely, and shall execute justice and righteousness in the land. In his days Judah will be saved, and Israel will dwell securely. And this is the nation by which he will be called: 'The Lord is our righteousness'" (Jer 23:5–6).

## BLESSING THE NATIONS THROUGH A PERSON: THE SPIRIT

The people of the Old Testament did not experience the permanent indwelling Spirit that the people of God would come to know in the first century. If the Spirit came upon someone, it was generally for a brief period of time to provide empowerment for a particular task; the Spirit enacts God's plan to gather the nations through Israel.[24] This is especially true in the words of Isaiah, Ezekiel, and Joel.

The Lord promises Israel he will pour his "Spirit upon your offspring and my blessing upon your descendants" (Isa 44:3). This would be a moment of great blessing and comfort (Isa 44:2). After describing the departure of the glory of God from the temple, Ezekiel states God will bring his people back from captivity. The Lord God says, "I will give them one heart, and a new spirit I will put within them. I will remove the heart of stone from

---

missionary effort" (*The Missionary Message of the Old Testament*, 64). Rowley also writes that Deutero-Isaiah believed that Israel's calling involved missionary activity (76).

23. Matthew cites Isaiah 53:4 as being fulfilled in the healing work of Jesus (Matt 8:14–17).

24. Duane A. Garrett, *Hosea, Joel* (Nashville: Broadman & Holman, 1997), 368.

their flesh and give them a heart of flesh, that they may walk in my statutes and keep my rules and obey them" (Ezek 11:19-20).

The prophet receives a peculiar vision of a valley of bones, representing Israel (37:11). After he obeys the command to prophesy over the bones, the breath (Spirit) of the Lord brings them to life (37:4-10). What was God's purpose for this strange sight? Though Israel thought all hope was gone since she lost the land and the temple, God was going to bring restoration by placing his Spirit within her and returning her to the land (37:14). Like many prophecies that have partial fulfillments on the way to total completion, this one is no exception. The end of the Babylonian exile partially fulfilled this promise, but Israel still waits for its complete fulfillment.[25] For additional understanding, we need to give attention to another passage.

One of the most significant texts related to God's mission and the Spirit comes from Joel. Preceding the cosmological wonders associated with the day of the Lord (Joel 2:30-31), Joel writes that a time will arrive when the Lord will show no discrimination with his Spirit toward his people:

> And it shall come to pass afterward, that I will pour out my Spirit on all flesh; your sons and your daughters shall prophesy, your old men shall dream dreams, and your young men shall see visions. Even on the male and female servants in those days I will pour out my Spirit. (Joel 2:28-29)[26]

While the prophets addressed different matters related to the eschatological outpouring and the people of God, their views complement one another. Garrett writes:

> The gift of the Spirit connotes direct experience with God, as in Joel, as well as the grace that enables his people to love God from the heart, as in Ezekiel. It also is the distinctive sign and mark of membership in the new people of God, as in Isaiah. In short, the coming age would be an age marked by the presence of the Spirit.[27]

---

25. Charles H. H. Scobie, *The Ways of Our God: An Approach to Biblical Theology* (Grand Rapids: Eerdmans, 2003), 276.

26. This passage reflects the fulfillment of Moses's desire (Num 11:29).

27. Garrett, *Hosea, Joel*, 368. See also Jeremiah 32:36-41 for a variation on 31:31-34.

Taken as a whole, the prophets establish an important pneumatological foundation for future revelation. When the Spirit arrives at Pentecost, the New Testament gives particular attention to Joel's prophecy noting the last days have arrived, the day of the Lord is near. The Spirit comes to bless, comfort, guide, and empower God's people to be his witnesses among the nations, with the hope they may be judged by the Spirit and Word, repent, and experience God's relational blessings as they participate in God's mission to the nations.

## BLESSING THE NATIONS THROUGH A PROMISE: NEW COVENANT

Israel's history involved several covenant renewal events (Exod 34; Deuteronomy; Josh 23–24; 1 Sam 12; 2 Chr 29–31; 2 Chr 34:3–7). These periods of repentance and recommitment were never fully able to transform the people. Given time, Israel would return to her wicked ways. A change of heart was needed. While the ideas connected with the new covenant are expressed throughout the Old Testament, the wording "new covenant" is only found in Jeremiah.[28]

> Behold, the days are coming, declares the LORD, when I will make a new covenant with the house of Israel and the house of Judah, not like the covenant that I made with their fathers on the day when I took them by the hand to bring them out of the land of Egypt, my covenant that they broke, though I was their husband, declares the LORD. For this is the covenant that I will make with the house of Israel after those days, declares the LORD: I will put my law within them, and I will write it on their hearts. And I will be their God, and they shall be my people. And no longer shall each one teach his neighbor and each his brother, saying, "Know the LORD," for they shall all know me, from the least of them to the greatest, declares the LORD. For I will forgive their iniquity, and I will remember their sin no more. (Jer 31:31–34)

What is *new* about the new covenant as God's mission unfolds in the world? This covenant is a response to Israel's ongoing rebellion toward God.

---

28. F. B. Huey, *Jeremiah, Lamentations* (Nashville: Broadman & Holman, 1993), 281.

The people's hearts will be transformed, and then they will be faithful to the covenant. The new covenant changes the infidelity problem. It upholds God's standards but provides the ability for the people to remain faithful. God's standard will be upon their hearts. The new covenant will provide a new relationship between God and his people. While teachers will not be discarded, imperfect leaders (i.e., mediators) will be gone. Throughout Israel's history, her mediators became corrupt, and their corruption influenced the nation as a whole. Only true believers will know God and thus be part of his community of people. Hearts will be changed and no room will be available for the unregenerate. The new covenant will not be the old covenant 2.0, but *new*, with a new arrangement between God and his people.[29]

Ezekiel 34–37 addresses the notion of God's restored people governed and shepherded by an eternal Davidic king (Ezek 37:24–25). God's people will one day walk in obedience to his rules and statutes under an eternal covenant of peace. He will again dwell among his people and then the nations will know that he is "the Lord who sanctifies Israel" (Ezek 37:26–28). This new covenant cleanses God's people and affects them in such a way that the nations are influenced by such grace. It is possible, unlike other prophets, Ezekiel may not have foreseen the nations entering into a relationship with Israel's God. Regardless, his vision was universal in scope. The repeated use of "then they will know" in Ezekiel 34–37 demonstrates the inevitability of the nations' knowledge of God when God is fully with his people.[30] Ezekiel concludes his book with a future vision of a new temple filled with God's glory (Ezek 43) and God dwelling among his people in a city named "The Lord is There" (Ezek 48:35).

The New Testament writers apply new covenant language and fulfillment to Messiah (Matt 26:26–29; Luke 22:20). As Jeremiah predicted a transformed people, the Gospels note the significance of God's work on behalf of, and within, his people. Such work will be seated within the eschatological timeframe of both the restoration of God's people and the extension of his good news to the nations. The new covenant is made, but it made for both the welfare of Israel *and* the nations.

---

29. Gentry and Wellum, *Kingdom through Covenant*, 483–530.
30. Wright, *The Mission of God*, 338.

## MOVEMENT OF THE GENTILES: ESCHATOLOGICAL INGATHERING

Though a day of judgment comes for the nations, the vision of the prophets is one whereby the nations align themselves with Torah and YHWH is their God. His name will be great and feared among the nations (Mal 1:11, 14). Salvation will come to the repentant. Scholars for decades have described the primary understanding of the outworking of God's mission in the Old Testament as centripetal acts. Instead of Israel going to the nations with Torah, the nations are pulled to Jerusalem.[31] The timing of this event is to occur at the end of days. Isaiah describes this eschatological movement of the nations to the holy city:

> It shall come to pass in the latter days that the mountain of the house of the LORD shall be established as the highest of the mountains, and shall be lifted up above the hills; and all the nations shall flow to it, and many peoples shall come, and say: "Come, let us go up to the mountain of the LORD, to the house of the God of Jacob, that he may teach us his ways and that we may walk in his paths." For out of Zion shall go forth the law, and the word of the LORD from Jerusalem. (Isa 2:1–3)

Perhaps one of the most scandalous verses in the prophets, related to the gentile ingathering, is found in Isaiah. The prophet not only shows God's grace and compassion toward Israel's enemies, but makes them equivalent with her:

> In that day there will be a highway from Egypt to Assyria, and Assyria will come into Egypt, and Egypt into Assyria, and the Egyptians will worship with the Assyrians. In that day Israel will be the third with Egypt and Assyria, a blessing in the midst of the earth, whom the LORD of hosts has blessed, saying, "Blessed be Egypt my people, and Assyria the work of my hands, and Israel my inheritance." (Isa 19:23–25)[32]

---

31. As noted in chapter two, Elijah (1 Kgs 17:8–24), Jonah, and Isaiah 66:18–21 are the few exceptions to the norm and reflect centrifugal motion.

32. Wright describes this passage as "one of the most breathtaking pronouncements" in the Prophets and "certainly one of the missiologically most significant texts in the Old Testament" (Wright, *Mission of God*, 236).

Throughout Israel's history, she resided on the land bridge between Egypt and Assyria and felt their invasions and wrath. Yet, the prophet sees a day when the wicked nations will become the people of YHWH alongside of Israel!

During that day, the Lord will make a celebration for all nations in Jerusalem (Isa 25:6). He "will swallow up death forever; and the Lord GOD will wipe away tears from all faces, and the reproach of his people he will take away from all the earth" (Isa 25:8; cf. 1 Cor 15:54; Rev 21:4). Given such great news, it is no wonder the prophet extends the invitation from the Lord: "Turn to me and be saved, all the end of the earth! For I am God, and there is no other … To me every knee shall bow, every tongue shall swear allegiance" (Isa 45:22–23; cf. Rom 14:11; Phil 2:10–11).

Zechariah paints a picture of the gentiles aching to get to Jerusalem to obtain blessing from God. So eager, they are quick to find the nearest Jew and follow his or her lead to the city:

> Thus says the LORD of hosts: Peoples shall yet come, even the inhabitants of many cities. The inhabitants of one city shall go to another, saying, 'Let us go at once to entreat the favor of the LORD and to seek the LORD of hosts; I myself am going.' Many peoples and strong nations shall come to seek the LORD of hosts in Jerusalem and to entreat the favor of the LORD. Thus says the LORD of hosts: In those days ten men from the nations of every tongue shall take hold of the robe of a Jew, saying, 'Let us go with you, for we have heard that God is with you.' (Zech 8:20–23)

This eschatological reality observed by Micah is a time when the nations will desire to learn from the Lord.

> It shall come to pass in the latter days that the mountain of the house of the LORD shall be established as the highest of the mountains, and it shall be lifted up above the hills; and peoples shall flow to it, and many nations shall come, and say: "Come, let us go up to the mountain of the LORD, to the house of the God of Jacob, that he may teach us his ways and that we may walk in his paths." For out of Zion shall go forth the law, and the word of the LORD from Jerusalem. (Mic 4:1–2)

This gentile ingathering was to occur during the latter days. Though Israel was to live out God's kingdom ethic, it would be God who would bring the nations to Israel and thus himself (Isa 56:5).[33] This centripetal movement is related to God's initiative and his relationship with Israel. Both parties were active in the work. Israel manifests life in God's kingdom as God draws the nations to relationship with himself. While the New Testament will describe the centrifugal movement of God's people to the nations, again, both parties are involved in the process. God remains the one who brings the nations to himself, though his means is primarily found in his people's apostolic efforts while displaying kingdom life to a watching world.

## BLESSING THE NATIONS THROUGH JUDGMENT: DAY OF THE LORD

The prophets used the phrase "the day of the Lord" to describe a near and/or distant future event when God would bring about radical change to the present reality. The events leading to the day of the Lord sometimes arrived in stages.[34] The day meant judgment and destruction of evil to be followed by peace and restoration for the righteous. This new ultimate reality would be eternally fixed. The day of the Lord meant cosmological changes and should be feared (Joel 2:31; Amos 5:18). Both Israel and the nations would experience the day of the Lord. No one escapes (Isa 2:12; Zech 14:1–3). The day was also in close proximity to the recipients of the prophets' messages (Ezek 30:3–5; Obad 15–16; Zeph 1:14–16).

Though such judgment is foretold, God has no pleasure in the death of the wicked (Ezek 18:21–23). Nations can avoid the destruction through repentance (Jer 18:7–8). The Ninevites response to Jonah's message is an example of God's grace to the wicked (Jonah 3:10). Joel notes destruction is not the result for all: "Everyone who calls on the name of the LORD shall be saved," and "in Mount Zion and in Jerusalem there shall be those who escape, as the LORD has said, and among the survivors shall be those whom the LORD calls" (Joel 2:31–32). Malachi noted the Lord would "send you Elijah

---

33. Andreas J. Köstenberger and Peter T. O'Brien, *Salvation to the Ends of the Earth: A Biblical Theology of Mission* (Downers Grove, IL: InterVarsity Press, 2001), 42.

34. Andrew E. Hill and John H. Walton, *A Survey of the Old Testament* (Grand Rapids: Zondervan Publishing House, 1991), 408.

the prophet before the great and awesome day of the LORD" (Mal 4:5).[35] His coming would be to change the hearts of God's people, "lest I come and strike the land with a decree of utter destruction" (Mal 4:6). Wright sums up the hope for the nations in view of the day: "There is no favoritism in God's dealings with Israel and the nations. All stand under YHWH's judgments. All can turn to YHWH and find his mercy."[36] The prophets' message of judgment was an example of grace through warning. The day would soon arrive, but the present was a day of hope found in salvation.

## BLESSING OF THE NATIONS THROUGH RESTORATION: DAY OF THE LORD

Coupled with the prophets' messages of sin and judgment was the message of hope in a global and eternal restoration to come. Israel would become the blessed people, but so would the nations around her. The cosmic corruption that followed the fall would be replaced with a renewed reality.

Though Israel was in the depths of despair, Isaiah notes that a remnant of God's people were left, and "a shoot from the stump of Jesse" shall bear fruit. God will place his spirit on the Davidic ruler who will be filled with righteousness and faithfulness. Even the animal kingdom will be transformed by his rule, and "the earth shall be full of the knowledge of the Lord as the waters cover the sea" (Isa 11:1–9; cf. Hab 2:14). This Anointed One will bring good news, healing, and comfort. Honor and everlasting joy shall be brought to God's people, who will be called the priest of the LORD, and receive his everlasting covenant (Isa 61:1–9). The Lord will "create new heavens and a new earth, and the former things shall not be remembered." Weeping will not be heard in Jerusalem, and her inhabitants will be healthy and prosperous (Isa 65:17–25).

Amos declared the booth of David will be rebuilt and the fortunes of Israel restored (Amos 9:11, 14). The Lord will "plant them on their land, and they shall never again be uprooted out of the land" (Amos 9:15). During the day of the Lord, those in Mount Zion will escape God's wrath (Obad 17). Zephaniah describes a time when the Lord will take away his judgment

---

35. The New Testament notes that John the Baptist was the Elijah who arrived in the first century (Matt 11:14).

36. Wright, *The Mission of God*, 462.

from Israel and remove her enemies. He will be in their midst, and they "shall never again fear evil" (Zeph 2:15). His love will bring peace to his people and will rejoice over them. The prophet describes a time when, after the Lord changes the speech of the nations "to a pure speech, that all of them may call upon the name of the LORD" (Zeph 3:9), he will gather together his people, make them renowned and praised throughout the world, and have their fortunes restored (Zeph 3:14-20). Joel looks to a day when the area around Jerusalem "shall drip sweet wine, and the hills shall flow with milk," and "a fountain shall come forth from the house of the LORD" (Joel 3:18). The enemies of Israel (i.e., Egypt and Edom) shall be desolate, but "Judah shall be inhabited forever, and Jerusalem to all generations" (Joel 3:19-20). Zechariah explains Israel's righteous and humble king will arrive to save and protect his people (Zech 9:9, 16). He will come in great power and bring about cosmic and earthly changes. The end result is that "the LORD will be king over all the earth," and nations will come annually to Jerusalem "to worship the king, the LORD of hosts, and to keep the Feast of Booths" (Zech 14:6-9, 16). The Prophets testify consistently to the coming acceptance of God by the nations.[37] Not only would the peoples of the world experience grace from God, but this would also result in their transformation and healing.

## CONCLUSION

Within the prophets' messages is an anticipated and promised day of hope. God is faithful to his promises and true to his mission. He will not abandon Israel to her enemies. Though their messages address matters related to sin and judgment, the prophets call God's people to covenantal faithfulness. A day will come when not only Israel will be restored to the land with a Davidic Servant-King and filled with the Spirit of God, but her enemies will submit to her and her God. This king will bless both Israel and the nations. He will yoke them together under Torah. All things will be restored for eternity.

---

37. Allan J. McNicol, *The Conversion of the Nations in Revelation* (New York: T&T Clark, 2011), 88.

## REFLECTION QUESTIONS

1. How would you describe the difference between historical incorporation and eschatological ingathering?

2. What did the temple signify in Israel and why was it so important to God's mission?

3. How does the Davidic covenant build upon the Abrahamic covenant?

4. What was the significance of the Spirit filling God's people in the last days?

# CHAPTER 5

# Mission in the Writings

THE WRITINGS COMPRISE the latter section of the Hebrew Scriptures and attempt to show how the people of God were to live in a variety of circumstances.[1] This section draws attention to the application of Torah to life. The Psalms reveal Israel's individual and corporate worship as the nations observe the praise of God's people and are invited to participate.[2] Proverbs, Ecclesiastes, Lamentations, and Song of Songs show the value of wisdom and fear of God, the place of life's deepest questions, the role of national mourning, and the place of love and sex in courtship and marriage. Characters such as Ruth, Daniel, Esther, and Job reflect the challenges of difficult circumstances when life does not make sense and enemies appear to thrive. Ezra-Nehemiah and Chronicles describe God's faithfulness throughout Israel's history and the fulfillment of his promises as the people return to the land from captivity to restore Jerusalem and the temple before the day of the Lord. The Writings often reflect a worldview that is contrary to their gentile contemporaries, and are therefore especially relevant to a discussion of mission and the nations in the Hebrew Scriptures.[3]

---

1. These works include: Psalms, Job, Proverbs, Ruth, Song of Songs, Ecclesiastes, Lamentations, Esther, Daniel, Ezra-Nehemiah, and Chronicles.

2. For example, commenting on the global appeal of Psalm 96, Leonard P. Maré writes, "Salvation has been announced and enacted in Israel's worship. Now it is being made effective in a new social reality also in the lives of those outside the Covenant people, by this invitation to join in celebrating the King. The nations are called to participate in the gift of salvation." Leonard P. Maré, "Israel's Praise as Enactment of the Gospel: Psalm 96 in Missiological Context," *Missionalia* 34, no. 2/3 (Aug–Nov 2006): 402.

3. Christopher J. H. Wright, "Old Testament Theology of Mission," in A. Scott Moreau, ed., *Evangelical Dictionary of World Missions* (Grand Rapids: Baker Books, 2000), 708.

## BLESSING THE NATIONS THROUGH
## ISRAEL'S INFLUENCE

The Writings are not shy when it comes to the topic of God's acceptance of the gentiles. Though Torah forbids the entrance of a Moabite into the Lord's assembly (Deut 23:3), an exception is found in the Book of Ruth. It was likely that through the witness of Naomi and her sons Ruth recognized the significance of Israel's God and made her declaration of faith (1:16). After marrying Boaz, Ruth gives birth to Obed, the grandfather of King David. The inclusion of Moabite blood in the Davidic line, and thus messianic genealogy, communicates even Israel's worst enemies are welcomed and received by her God.

While in captivity, Israel bears witness to the God of the nations. God gave Daniel, Hananiah, Mishael, and Azariah the ability to grow in wisdom, learning, and skill regarding Babylonian culture and society (Dan 1:17–20). After interpreting a dream, Nebuchadnezzar paid homage to Daniel's ability and his God (Dan 2:46–47). Though Daniel and his acquaintances would experience great persecution at the hands of Babylon, their testimony to God would echo in the ears of their tormentors for years to follow (Dan 3:24–30; 6). Nebuchadnezzar's declaration would have made an impression on his officials and other observers:

> I blessed the Most High, and praised and honored him who lives forever, for his dominion is an everlasting dominion, and his kingdom endures from generation to generation; all the inhabitants of the earth are accounted as nothing, and he does according to his will among the host of heaven and among the inhabitants of the earth; and none can stay his hand or say to him, "What have you done?" (Dan 4:34–35)

It is in the context of the Book of Daniel that the reader receives divine confirmation of the statements made by Nebuchadnezzar. While Israel could agree with such declaration, it is easy to imagine she could overlook its significance having been spoken by a gentile oppressor.[4] However,

---

4. Torah noted God's mission is sometimes revealed and truth communicated through unbelieving gentiles as found in the story of Balak and Balaam (Num 22–24).

Daniel would experience a revelation which would clarify any doubt regarding God's reign over Israel and the other nations.

## BLESSING THE NATIONS THROUGH SOVEREIGNTY

During the first year of Belshazzar's rule, Daniel records a vision in which the Ancient of Days extends to the Son of Man "dominion and glory and a kingdom, that all peoples, nations, and languages should serve him," with this reign and kingdom being everlasting and "one that shall not be destroyed" (Dan 7:13-14). Daniel is allowed to see a vision of God's rule that includes not only the incorporation of the Hebrews into God's kingdom but the gentiles as well. Such would have been an astounding vision, given at a time when the gentiles had wreaked great havoc on Israel. But before this event would take place, a day of judgment would come when Israel would be delivered (Dan 12:1-3).

The Writings reminds readers God is sovereign over creation. He will one day bring every deed to judgment (Eccl 12:14). The hearts of people lie open before him (Prov 15:11; Eccl 11:9). The die may be cast, but its outcome is from the Lord (Prov 16:33; Esth 9:23-28). Though people make plans, the Lord is the one who establishes their steps (Prov 16:9). Nothing escapes his rule: "The Lord has made everything for its purpose" (Prov 16:4; Esth 4:14). The kings of this world are no match to him, for he turns their hearts wherever he desires to accomplish his mission (Prov 21:1). Wisdom, understanding, and counsel are no match for the Lord, either. He even brings about battlefield victories regardless of the might of the army (Prov 21:30-31). What he has promised will come to pass, for "every word of God proves true" (Prov 30:5). Such knowledge would bring great comfort to Israel, but also served as a note that God would never forget his words regarding the gentiles. His mission to redeem and restore remains regardless of Israel's circumstances.

Several psalms (47, 97, 98, 99) note the sovereign reign of God over the nations. His rule brings music, excitement, and joy (Ps 47:1). His approach to subduing the nations results in "the princes of the peoples" gathering "as the people of the God of Abraham" (Ps 47:9). Again, here the promise that all nations would be blessed through Abraham is fulfilled (Gen 12:1-3).

God, though maintaining a unique relationship with Israel, is God of the entire world.[5]

Why is this grand inclusion of all peoples possible? It is because of God's character and love for Israel. The Lord has not hidden himself from the nations but has made known his salvation to them. His relationship with the house of Israel results in all the ends of the earth seeing his salvation (Ps 98:2–3). Knowledge of the relationship between Israel and her God is designed to persuade the gentiles that he is sovereign.[6]

Even in Job, a book some scholars find difficult to connect with the larger biblical narrative, the mission of God is revealed. In a fascinating study, Tim J. Davy notes that rather than attempting to fit the text into the biblical and historical storyline, Job stands apart from it and speaks into it.[7] In Job, the very mission of God is at stake as revealed with Satan's question (Job 1:9). Does God simply buy the loyalty of his people through blessing?[8] Davy argues the book vindicates "both Job and Yahweh and, in doing so, vindicates the *mission Dei* itself."[9] God is sovereign and working out his purpose in the world, even when his creation does not, and will never, understand the reasons for his actions.

The Writings note that God's hand works to preserve his people even when hope seems lost (Esth 4:14). Though Jerusalem is destroyed and lonely among the nations (Lam 1:1), his steadfast love and mercies are eternal. Because of this consistency of his faithfulness to his character and word, Israel will hope in him (Lam 3:22–24). The Redeemer of Israel is alive and able to see the hearts of his people in times of trouble (Job 16:19; 19:25). Though struggles and difficulties come, oftentimes through judgment, hope and restoration follow.

---

5. Tremper Longman III, *Psalms: An Introduction and Commentary* (Downers Grove, IL: InterVarsity Press, 2014), 208.

6. Martin-Achard, *A Light to the Nations*, 59.

7. Tim J. Davy, *The Book of Job and the Mission of God: A Missional Reading* (Eugene, OR: Pickwick, 2020), 128.

8. Davy, *The Book of Job and the Mission of God*, 86, 125, 127.

9. Davy, *The Book of Job and the Mission of God*, 223.

## BLESSING THE NATIONS THROUGH
## RESTORATION AND RECONSTRUCTION

The Hebrew Scriptures end with the book of Chronicles.[10] After tracing Israel's history beginning with Adam (1 Chr 1:1), the book concludes by recalling Babylonian captivity (2 Chr 36:17–21) and Cyrus's decree to allow Israel to return to their land (2 Chr 36:22–23). Jeremiah's prophecy (Jer 29:10–11; cf. 2 Chr 36:21–22) saw fulfillment during the reign of Cyrus, king of Persia (Ezra 1:1). After conquering Babylon, Cyrus made the following decree:

> The LORD, the God of heaven, has given me all the kingdoms of the earth, and he has charged me to build him a house at Jerusalem, which is in Judah. Whoever is among you of all his people, may his God be with him, and let him go up to Jerusalem, which is in Judah, and rebuild the house of the LORD, the God of Israel—he is the God who is in Jerusalem. And let each survivor, in whatever place he sojourns, be assisted by the men of his place with silver and gold, with goods and with beasts, besides freewill offering for the house of God that is in Jerusalem. (Ezra 1:2–4)

This is a very important passage regarding God's mission. Though Assyria had destroyed the northern tribes of Israel in 722 BC and Babylon the southern tribes in 587 BC, the people of God had to return to the land and reestablish themselves as a nation before the day of the Lord. The book of Ezra-Nehemiah marks a significant moment in God's plan of redemption and restoration.[11]

In this book, the exiles return from captivity and resettle the land and rebuild the temple and Jerusalem. The temple is completed during the days of Darius (Ezra 6:14–15) and the priests and Levites are restored to service (Ezra 6:18). The repopulating of Jerusalem and rebuilding the wall around the city marked the beginning of the reestablishment of the people as a nation. The political and social structures would eventually develop for Israel. Artaxerxes allowed Nehemiah to return to Jerusalem and, with provisions, repair the city wall. Nehemiah recognized God's guidance in

---

10.  1 and 2 Chronicles are considered a single book in the Hebrew Scriptures.

11.  Ezra and Nehemiah are considered a single book in the Hebrew Scriptures.

the matter (Neh 2:1–8). The wall was rebuilt at great speed. The joy experienced on dedication day was heard far away (Neh 12:43). While it took time for Israel to return to the standards of Ezra and Nehemiah (Ezra 10; Neh 13), this book closes with the hopeful expectation that the people of God will serve him faithfully. He has been faithful to his word; will Israel be faithful to her word? Soon, the Davidic king will arrive, provide deliverance, and restore all things.

## BLESSING THE NATIONS: INVITATION THROUGH PRAISE

As God's image-bearers fill the earth and bring glory to his name, their worship not only strengthens their kingdom community but bears witness to the divine-human relationship and blessings received from God. In the New Testament, Paul's words to the Corinthians acknowledged the influence of the worshiping community before unbelievers (1 Cor 14:24–25). The people of God have always been a people of praise while inviting a watching world to join them. Several of the psalms reveal that though Israel was God's particular people, they were not to be isolated from the nations. Their worship was both to reflect the grace they received and an expectation that others would come to glorify her God. The book of Psalms portrays a God with no geographical boundaries. He is not limited to any space in his creation and has an international vision. The mission of Israel and God's all-encompassing plan for the nations is a major theme of Psalms.[12]

Possibly sung during the harvest season, the psalmist calls upon God for corporate blessings in Psalm 67. The desire is for God's face to shine upon his people (Ps 67:1). Referencing the Aaronic blessing of Numbers 6:24–26, the writer reminds Israel that what she receives from God is not to be consumed for selfish gain. Relationship brings blessings, but blessings are to point the nations to God. The psalmist asks for God's favor that his "way may be known on the earth" and his "saving power among all nations" (Ps 67:2). Israel is to desire that all the peoples of the earth would praise her God and find delight and joy in relationship with him (Ps 67:3–4, 5).

---

12. Mark J. Boda, "Declare his Glory among the Nations," in Stanley E. Porter and Cynthia Long Westfall, eds., *Christian Mission: Old Testament Foundations and New Testament Developments* (Eugene, OR: Pickwick, 2011), 26.

The book of Psalms also describes the vision of all the nations worshiping the God of Israel. Because there is no god like YHWH, "all the nations you have made shall come and worship before you, O Lord, and shall glorify your name" (Ps 86:8–9). The gods of the nations are worthless idols (Ps 96:5). Israel is to "declare his glory among the nations, his marvelous works among all the peoples!" (Ps 96:3). The nations are to know that God reigns and judges the nations with equity, righteousness, and faithfulness (Ps 96:10, 13). The nations are called to "ascribe to the Lord glory and strength" and "bring an offering, and come into his courts!" (Ps 96:7, 8). The language of verse 7 ("families of the peoples") is an echo of God's promise to Abraham that all nations would be blessed through him (Gen 12:3).[13]

Psalm 87 is a beautiful picture of God's love for Zion and the people found there. What is most surprising is that the psalmist foretells a day when some of Israel's most notorious enemies are granted citizenship in the city. The Lord records and registers the inhabitants (Ps 87:6). Glorious things are spoken of the holy city (Ps 87:3). What is found in these grand conversations? The nations that know the Lord include Rahab, possibly a reference to Egypt, Babylon, Philistia, Tyre, and the ends of the earth, represented by Cush (Ps 87:4). On that day, it will be said of the nations, "this one and that one were born in her" (Ps 87:5).

At a time when Zion was experiencing great distress, the psalmist asks that his prayer be answered. Trouble has come, possibly at the hands of Israel's enemies. Yet, found in the central poem of Psalm 102 (vv. 12–22), the writer is able to acknowledge that the Lord is eternally sovereign, and a day is coming when the distressed will be set free (Ps 102:12, 20). Instead of describing the destruction of Israel's enemies, the psalmist notes that on that day peoples and kingdoms will gather together to worship the Lord (Ps 102:22).[14] The nations are exhorted to praise the Lord enthusiastically (Ps 117:1).[15] God is gracious, good, and merciful to all he has made (Ps 145:8–9). His righteous people are to tell of his works "to the children of man" (Ps 145:10–12). In addition to Israel, "Kings of the earth and all peoples,

---

13. Longman, *Psalms*, 342.

14. Kidner notes the language of peoples and kingdoms going to Zion "is radiantly presented in Isaiah 60–62, and further interpreted in Revelation 21." See Derek Kidner, *Psalms 73–150* (Downers Grove, IL: IVP Academic, 1975), 395.

15. Paul draws from this passage to support his ministry to the gentiles (Romans 15:11).

princes and all rulers of the earth! Young men and maidens together, old men and children!" are to praise the Lord (Ps 148:11–12, 14). And if this list is not comprehensive enough, Psalms ends with the declaration that "everything that has breath" is to praise the Lord (Ps 150:6).

While Psalms is filled with doxology and doctrine, it is a book that reminds Israel of both her privileged position among the nations *and* her responsibility before the nations. The Psalter served as a perennial reminder that her God was also the God of all the nations. His reign was not limited to a strip of land east of the Mediterranean. He created all and ruled over all. Therefore, it should not come as a surprise that Psalms concludes with such a grand invitation for everything that breathes to praise God. Could it be that John had the fulfillment of Psalm 150 in mind when he wrote:

> And I heard every creature in heaven and on earth and under the earth and in the sea, and all that is in them, saying, "To him who sits on the throne and to the Lamb be blessing and honor and glory and might forever and ever!" (Rev 5:13)[16]

## BLESSING THE NATIONS THROUGH A PERSON: GOD'S ANOINTED REIGNS

Psalm 2 notes the relationship of the nations to the Lord's Son. This messianic passage is rooted in the Davidic covenant (2 Sam 7:1–17) and finds ultimate fulfillment in Jesus.[17] God laughs at the kings and rulers who attempt to stand against his anointed. He gives the nations to his Son who will rule over his enemies with a rod of iron. However, such judgment and destruction are not inevitable. The rulers of the nations are warned to be wise and serve the Lord and kiss the Son (Ps 2:10–12a), because "blessed are all who

---

16. Kidner quotes Revelation 5:13 after his exposition of Psalm 150. See Kidner, *Psalms 73–150*, 529.

17. Derek Kidner notes though the New Testament never quotes this psalm as messianic, its close connection with other possible messianic passages found in Isaiah (i.e., Isa 11:1–5; 60–62) makes it messianic. He writes, "As a royal psalm it prayed for the reigning king, and was a strong reminder of his high calling; yet it exalted this so far beyond the humanly attainable (e.g., in speaking of his reign as endless) as to suggest for its fulfilment no less a person than the Messiah, not only to Christian thinking but to Jewish," Derek Kidner, *Psalms 1–72* (Downers Grove, IL: IVP Academic, 1973), 273.

take refuge in him" (Ps 2:12). The kings of this world do not have to stand against the king of Israel. They are not obligated to be his enemies, but may come to him and find relationship and blessing.

In a similar fashion, Psalm 72 reveals the desire of the writer for God to give the king universal reign. His dominion is to be to the ends of the earth (Ps 72:8). Blessings and grace are to be upon this royal son that he may judge with righteousness and provide deliverance and care for the needy and poor (Ps 72:2, 4, 12). The vision includes the kings of the world streaming to Jerusalem with tribute, service, and paying him homage (Ps 72:10–11, 15). It is through his reign that people will find blessings, and "all nations call him blessed" (Ps 72:17). It is if God works his mission through this king that the whole earth will be filled with God's glory (Ps 72:19).

## BLESSING THE NATIONS THROUGH A PERSON: GOD'S ANOINTED SUFFERS

Psalm 22 reveals the cry of the psalmist who suffers greatly at the hands of his enemies while his prayers remain unanswered (Ps 22:1–2). Even though he is grieved, he trusts in God, and his message of good news extends to the nations. While the mission of God in this passage finds fulfillment in the crucified Messiah (Matt 27:34–35, 43, 46; Mark 15:24, 29; Luke 23:34; John 19:24; Heb 2:12), it also manifests itself in an often overlooked part of this text. After noting his confidence in the Lord who provides deliverance, the psalmist states, "all the ends of the earth shall remember and turn to the LORD, and all the families of the nations shall worship before you. For kingship belongs to the LORD, and he rules over the nations" (Ps 22:27–28).

This text, like the rest of Psalms, lacks clarity regarding the method by which the nations come to God. The conversion of the nations does not rest on Israel's shoulders, but rather the impetus is on God.[18] God will accomplish the salvation of the nations by working through Israel, as seen in psalms such as 47 and 87.[19] This notion that the gentile ingathering will occur by the hand of the Lord seems to be in agreement with the message of

---

18. Miller, "The Gentiles in the Zion Hymns," 235.
19. Miller, "The Gentiles in the Zion Hymns," 236.

the prophets addressed in chapter 4. Regardless, what is evident is that one day the peoples of the world who bear the image of God will worship him.[20]

Though the Anointed One suffers greatly and is mocked by his tormentors (Ps 22:8; cf. Matt 27:43), he calls others to trust in the Lord who does not despise and hears (Ps 22:24). The messianic significance of this text cannot be passed over without comment. While the connection between the psalmist's suffering and the nations worshiping God is not as evident in this passage, the New Testament provides clarity. The Messiah's suffering for sin is part of the good news. God's judgment comes upon him, but so does the hope of resurrection. He suffers but trusts in God and receives the inheritance of the nations. It is this message that brings the nations into relationship with God.

## CONCLUSION

The Writings contain a rich array of literature. The collection provides Israel with exhortation and demonstration as to how the faithful are to live. God's faithfulness is shown throughout the historical narratives and in Israel's worship expressions. She must not forget her identity, heritage, and mission. The Writings reveal a God who is very much concerned with both Jews and gentiles and desires relationship with them. He is sovereign, restores Israel, and continues his mission through her. He is revealed as the God who has created all, oversees all, and is to be worshiped by all.

## REFLECTION QUESTIONS

1. List some ways (not described in this chapter) you think the Writings were to have an influence on the nations around Israel.

2. Were you aware of the amount of space in the book of Psalms that references the nations? What do you think may have been in the minds of ancient Israel when they sang those words?

3. How does the global attention found in Psalms affect your thinking about God's mission?

---

20. Wright, *The Mission of God*, 478.

# CHAPTER 6

# Mission in the Synoptics

TENSION BUILDS AS we trace the narrative from the garden through each Old Testament covenant.[1] The biblical narrative of God's plan and engagement with the world moves from crescendo to crescendo. Each covenant develops his relationship with his people and provides greater details regarding the restoration of all things. Following Babylonian captivity, Persia's rise to power, and Cyrus's decree, Israel is allowed to return to the land of their ancestors and rebuild Jerusalem (538 BC).

By the conclusion of the Old Testament, many of the promises of Abraham have been fulfilled. Israel is a numerous people. They are back in the land. Zerubbabel has rebuilt the second temple by 516/15 BC. But the head of the serpent has not been crushed, sin remains, and Israel still remains under the hand of her enemies. At this point in the story, the reader comes to a *diminuendo* in the movement.

The implied existence of the temple in Malachi (1:10; 3:1, 8), a reference to a term used for government officials during the Persian period (1:8), and discussion of the same sins as addressed by Ezra and Nehemiah have led some scholars to view the prophet as their contemporary in the mid-fifth century BC. Though many social, political, and cultural shifts would occur during the intertestamental period, it would be 400 years before the Evangelists would pen their books.

---

1. For a very helpful and extensive study of God's covenants see Peter J. Gentry and Stephen J. Wellum, *Kingdom through Covenant*.

The birth of the Baptist and Jesus moves the story of God's mission forward with a great but restrained force. Malachi concludes his work predicting Elijah's arrival before the "great and awesome day of the Lord" (Mal 4:5), and the Evangelists understood the Baptist to be the fulfillment of this prophecy (Matt 17:9–13; Luke 1:5–17; cf. Mark 1:4–8; John 1:6). Anticipation is heightened. Tension increases. Yet rather than a resounding cymbal crash, the Messiah arrives in a dirty manger.[2] Another climax to the story of God's mission has arrived, but not with the expected manifestations of grandeur and cosmic transformation.

God continues to unfold his plan to redeem and restore throughout the Synoptic Gospels. The pattern of purpose (sending to the world → proclaiming hope through judgment → entering relationship → receiving blessing) continues in this section and throughout the rest of the New Testament. This chapter will attempt to answer a few questions that have great bearing on God's mission: What was Jesus's relationship to the Jews and gentiles? Did Jesus have a mission to the gentiles? How do the Synoptics understand the future ingathering of the gentiles? Is the primary movement centripetal or centrifugal? What is the relation of the church to God's kingdom?

## THE DIVINE CONTINUITY BETWEEN
## THE OLD AND NEW TESTAMENTS

Jesus comes to do the will of the Father who sends him (Matt 26:39). He comes to "proclaim, to practice and to embody the good news of God's reign, not separately, but seamlessly."[3] Jesus's words and actions are a manifestation of what God desires. He is sent as God's beloved Son who brings pleasure to the Father (Matt 3:17; Mark 1:11; Luke 3:22). Without the fulfillment of the Law and Prophets (Matt 5:17–18) and the atoning sacrifice and resurrection (Matt 16:21–23), redemption (Matt 20:28) and restoration are impossibilities.

---

2. The majestic announcement with great pomp and circumstance did come, but only to some shepherds (Luke 2:13–14) and the magi who observed a single astronomical light (Matt 2:2). As will be noted, Matthew's attention to these gentiles from the East is the beginning of his theme related to the blessing of the nations.

3. Dean Flemming, *Recovering the Full Mission of God: A Biblical Perspective on Being, Doing and Telling* (Downers Grove, IL: IVP Academic, 2013), 78.

Without diminishing the significance of the atonement, an overlooked aspect of the person and work of the Son is that he served as a bridge of continuity between God working through his people in the Old and New Testaments. God's mission did not come to a hard conclusion with the coming of the Messiah, nor did Matthew's Gospel announce a new paradigm with a brand-new foundation. Rather, a transitory moment occurred. Jesus's mission continued the work of God. Köstenberger and O'Brien write, "The pattern of Jesus' mission thus bears a striking resemblance to that of Old Testament Israel which was called to be a mediatorial kingdom to the surrounding nations (cf. Exod. 19:6). Only *subsequent* to the cross and the resurrection was the gospel to be preached to all the nations (cf. Luke 24:46–47)."[4] What Israel failed to do, Jesus did and established a kingdom ethic for his disciples to follow under his reign. The New Testament notes that apart from Christ, the people of God will also fail in mission, but success is found in Christ working through his people. Jesus's approach to God's mission in the world involved *being, doing,* and *telling,* and was to be repeated through the church.[5] Jesus revealed continuity in the salvation-history paradigm and continued to foreshadow the eschatological reality of the gentile ingathering.

Israel failed to be the community of God's people. They did not live up to the Old Testament expectation to be royal priests, a holy nation, and a model to the world of what kingdom citizenship looked like. They failed to serve as a magnet, drawing the nations to Mount Zion to hear the word of God. As the true Israel, Jesus models servanthood before his disciples. After revealing to them what worship, prayer, preaching, healing, and exorcisms looked like, he sent them out to replicate his pattern (Luke 9:1–2; 10:9). These few men would quickly become leaders of his church that would soon be sent into the world with a message of hope while accomplishing more than Jesus himself accomplished (John 14:12).

---

4. Köstenberger and O'Brien, *Salvation to the Ends of the Earth,* 85.

5. For a fuller argument of being, doing, and telling, see Flemming, *Recovering the Full Mission of God.*

## FUTURE INGATHERING OF THE NATIONS

The birth of Jesus marked an end-time event that was intimately connected to the gentile ingathering. His coming and redemptive work inaugurated the final epoch before the eschaton.[6] He would restore the kingdom, but not immediately. Good news of the kingdom had to be proclaimed throughout the world (Act 1:6–7). For the first century believers, mission was not a secondary thought once the parousia did not occur. Rather, mission was an eschatological event designed to bring hope to the nations before the awesome day of the Lord.[7]

Before examining the post-Easter commissions in this chapter, a couple of related passages must be considered. Mark 13:10 notes before the end, "the gospel must first be proclaimed to all nations." Jesus foretold a day to come when his disciples would be arrested and persecuted as they bear witness before the gentiles (Matt 10:18). Following his anointing at Bethany, Jesus acknowledged a day when the gospel would be proclaimed in the whole world (Mark 14:9; Matt 26:13). The prophets foresaw a time when the nations would stream to Israel to hear Torah. Jesus's eschatological teaching was in line with the prophets, but the streaming would not necessary require the nations to leave their home and journey to the Middle East. Rather, God's royal priesthood and holy nation would take the blessings of Torah and the temple to the nations. The restriction of the mission to Israel was about to be removed, as the Hebrew Bible looked forward to in its anticipation of the salvation of the gentiles.[8] The Messiah had to come and die for his people prior to the ingathering of the nations. Both of these acts occurred in order to bring the gentiles into God's kingdom.[9]

It is well beyond the scope of this book to compare and critique eschatological views. The reader should be aware that diversity exists among scholars. Related to our topic, such views vary widely in relation to future matters regarding the nature and role of the church and Israel, the

---

6. Glasser, *Announcing the Kingdom*, 214. Luke will make a specific connection between the arrival of the Spirit and the last days as noted in Peter's sermon (Acts 2:17).

7. David J. Bosch, *Transforming Mission: Paradigm Shifts in Theology of Mission* (Maryknoll, NY: Orbis Books, 1991), 41.

8. Michael Bird, *Jesus and the Origins of the Gentile Mission* (New York: T&T Clark, 2007), 57.

9. Joachim Jeremias, *Jesus' Promise to the Nations*. Trans. S. H. Hooke (Naperville, IL: Alec R. Allenson, 1958), 73

promised land and temple, and the millennial reign of Christ. For example, some scholars argue for a future literal restoration of Israel as God's people, the movement of the gentiles *to* a restored temple in Jerusalem, and a thousand-year rule of Christ before the coming new heaven and earth. Other scholars note such matters are fulfilled in the church in her mission throughout the world today as she awaits Christ's return and then the judgment.

## JESUS AND THE GENTILE MISSION

Did Jesus have a mission that brought the gospel to the gentiles? Scholarship is divided over this question, with the majority believing he did not. While some agree a gentile mission may be found in the biblical text, others question its existence. Ferdinand Hahn is clear: "Jesus, indeed, performed his own works on Israel, and did not in any way carry on a 'mission to the gentiles.'" Yet, Hahn acknowledges Jesus's engagement with gentiles. His "activity extended to Samaria and far into gentile territory; gentiles came to him and showed an unconditional trust such as he had not met in Israel."[10] Though Jesus did make particularistic statements, it is clear he does not turn away gentiles who come to him.[11] Some think the answer to the question, at least in the Synoptics, may be found somewhere between those who find a gentile mission and those who do not.[12] It would be best to note while Jesus was primarily engaged with the Jews, he *foresaw* a mission that would embrace all nations and *prepared* his disciples for such work.[13] Eckhard J. Schnabel writes, "The Gospels indicated repeatedly that Jesus had contacts with gentiles, and that these contacts were not simply, or not always, accidental in nature but indeed a part of his mission that his disciples were to

---

10. Ferdinand Hahn, *Mission in the New Testament* (Naperville, IL: Alec R. Allenson, 1965), 39.

11. John D. Harvey writes such statements "must be weighed against aspects of his teaching and practice that suggest a more universal scope." John D. Harvey, "Mission in Jesus' Teaching," in *Mission in the New Testament: An Evangelical Approach*, ed. William J. Larkin Jr. and Joel F. Williams (Maryknoll, NY: Orbis Books, 1998), 38.

12. This is the perspective of Köstenberger and O'Brien in their discussion of mission in Mark's Gospel. *Salvation to the Ends of the Earth: A Biblical Theology of Mission* (Downers Grove, IL: InterVarsity Press, 2001), 73.

13. This statement stands in contradiction to the general consensus of historical Jesus scholarship. Michael F. Bird has written a book that disagrees with the general consensus, *Jesus and the Origins of the Gentile Mission*.

continue at a later time."[14] The Gospel writers have an "eschatological time frame in mind," and that is after the resurrection that the responsibility for taking the gospel to the gentiles resides with the disciples.[15]

The Synoptics find great importance in a gentile mission, but such work serves as a foretaste of what follows Jesus's ministry to Israel. But why is the universality kept quiet? The announcement of this global work was premature. Jesus first had to give his life as a ransom.[16] Though attention to the global advance comes near the conclusion of the Synoptic accounts, the evidence is clear: Messiah came for gentiles too.

Matthew's account of the nativity is quick to draw attention to the presence of gentile worshippers alongside of the Jews. The magi from the east come to offer gifts and their worship, for his star had been revealed to them, and they respond (Matt 2:2, 11). From the beginning, it is communicated that the coming of the Messiah is "good news of great joy that will be for all people" (Luke 2:10) and "a light for revelation to the gentiles, and for glory to your people Israel" (Luke 2:32; cf. Isa 42:6; 49:6; 52:10; 60:3).

Jesus makes journeys into gentile territories (Mark 5:1–20; 7:24, 31; Luke 9:52; 17:11; cf. John 4:4), but whenever he has interactions with gentiles, they generally occur as a result of gentile initiative. He marveled at the faith of the centurion at Capernaum (Matt 8:5–13; Luke 7:1–10), then described that many will come to the banquet table in the kingdom from the east and west, while the sons of the kingdom will be cast into darkness (Matt 8:5–13; Luke 7:1–10). He commended the Canaanite woman for her great faith (Matt 15:21–28) after an initially cold response to her plea for help (Mark 7:28; Matt 15:26). The Gerasene man is delivered from the demons (Mark 5:1–20), but Jesus denies the man's request and sends him home to share what the Lord has done (Mark 5:18–19). Ten lepers are cleansed, but only

---

14. Eckhard J. Schnabel, *Early Christian Mission: Jesus and the Twelve*, vol. 1 (Downers Grove, IL: InterVarsity Press, 2004), 333.

15. R. Geoffrey Harris, *Mission in the Gospels* (n.p.: Epworth, 2004), 50–51.

16. Karl Barth wrote: "The previous, historical, Israel had not yet run its course. ... The table had not been set. The guests could not yet be invited. Israel was not yet fully prepared to fulfill its eschatological mission. Aware of this "not yet," Jesus understood his mission to be—temporarily—to the lost sheep of the house of Israel." "An Exegetical Study of Matthew 28:16–20," in *The Theology of the Christian Mission*, ed. Gerald H. Anderson (Nashville: Abingdon, 1961), 65.

the Samaritan returned to praise God (Luke 17:11–19).[17] During the triumphal entry into Jerusalem, Matthew notes the fulfillment of Zechariah 9:9 (Matt 21:1–5). The context of this prophecy is that the king who rides into the city is the one who will "speak peace to the nations" (Zech 9:10). It was the centurion near the cross who acknowledges Jesus's divine connection (Matt 27:54; Mark 15:39; cf. Luke 23:47). Jesus's interactions with the gentiles foreshadow a post-resurrection period when the universal mission would occur before the day of the Lord.

As a matter of rebuke to Israel, Jesus draws attention to the gentiles. The queen of the South and the men of Nineveh will condemn Jesus's contemporaries due to their lack of faith in a much greater revelation than they experienced (Luke 11:29–32). The people's rage turns toward Jesus when he praises the widow of Zarephath and Naaman the Syrian above Israel (Luke 4:26–27). In his denunciation of Israel's unrepentant cities, Jesus notes the citizens of Sodom would have repented and remained if the works he did in Capernaum had been done in Sodom (Matt 11:20–24). Jesus's actions in the Court of the Gentiles at the temple connect with Isaiah's teaching about the nations. God's house was to be a "house of prayer for all the nations." However, the money changers of the first century turned it into a "den of robbers" (Mark 11:17; Matt 21:12–16; Luke 19:45–47; cf. John 2:14–16).

The gentiles, however, did not always receive commendation. Several indictments are extended toward them. It is the gentiles who act in ways that the Jews should not act. They only greet their brothers (Matt 5:47). When it comes to prayer, they believe their many words will cause the divine to respond (Matt 6:7). They worry about what they will eat, drink, and wear (Matt 6:31; Luke 12:29). They attempt to dominate one another (Mark 10:42; Luke 22:25). Their actions betray life in the kingdom to the point that one of the worst actions that could be brought against unrepentant Jews was to treat them as gentiles (Matt 18:17). Jesus teaches that while the gentiles act in such ungodly ways, God's people are to seek first his kingdom and righteousness (Matt 6:33; Luke 12:31).

---

17. Among others passages, Schnabel also includes as possible support for gentile interactions: the deaf-mute man of the Decapolis (Mark 7:32–37), the four thousand fed east of Galilee (Mark 8:1–10; Matt 15:32–39), other tenants of the vineyard (Matt 21:33–46; Mark 12:1–12; Luke 20:9–19), and the parable of the wedding (Matt 22:1–10; Luke 14:16–24). See Schnabel, *Jesus and the Twelve*, 343.

## BLESSING THE NATIONS THROUGH A
## PERSON: JESUS SENT TO THE JEWS

It is important to remember Jesus is born under the law, into a Jewish family. Jesus is described as the Messiah (Matt 1:1, 17; 26:63–64). His mission is to Israel (Matt 10:6; 15:24). He comes to save his people from their sins (Matt 1:21). The good news is to the Jew first (Rom 1:16; cf. Mark 7:26). It should come as no surprise the majority of Jesus's interactions in the Synoptics are with Jews, not gentiles.[18] Jesus clearly revealed he "was sent only to the lost sheep of the house of Israel" (Matt 15:24). Prior to the resurrection, he commands the Twelve to "go nowhere among the gentiles and enter no town of the Samaritans" (Matt 10:5–6). He is concerned with the poor (Luke 14:12–13). He is to rule Israel as the Davidic king (Matt 2:6; 19:28). He is God's servant (Matt 12:15–21). He fulfills the law (Matt 5:17).

Matthew's Gospel introduces Jesus as the one connected to Abraham's seed and David's eternal dynasty (Matt 1:1–17). He comes as the promised one who will bless the nations by his dominion over them. Irony is found in this Gospel, for Herod is described as the king of the Jews but fails to submit to the Messiah as gentiles from the East worship him (Matt 2:2). The persecution that follows drives Jesus and his family to Egypt. Their return to Israel fulfilled Hosea's prophecy identifying Jesus as the true Israel: "Out of Egypt I called my son" (Matt 2:15; cf. Hos 11:1). Jesus would accomplish the mission that was impossible for Israel and provide the means by which God's people would be able to take the message of hope through judgment to the nations before the day of the Lord.

Following his baptism and temptation, Jesus inaugurates his ministry by moving to Capernaum to fulfill a prophecy that tips a hat toward "Galilee of the gentiles" (Matt 4:15; cf. Isa 9:1, 2). Jesus begins teaching in the Galilean synagogues, healing the people, and casting out demons (Matt 4:23–24). At his public reading from Isaiah, he declares the text "fulfilled" and thus establishes continuity with the prophet and the messianic fulfillment: "The Spirit of the Lord is upon me, because he has anointed me to proclaim good news to the poor. He has sent me to proclaim liberty to the captives and

---

18. Michael Goheen notes "Jesus's task is in keeping with the prophetic promise that begins with the gathering and conversion of the Jews." *A Light to the Nations: The Missional Church and the Biblical Story* (Grand Rapids: Baker Academic, 2011), 81.

recovering of sight to the blind, to set at liberty those how are oppressed, to proclaim the year of the Lord's favor" (Luke 4:18–19; cf. Isa 61:1, 2).

The life and ministry of Jesus pointed to his divine nature and purpose. His teachings and miracles came with a surprising authority, oftentimes resulting in conflict with others. The people oppose Jesus's absolution of the paralytic as blasphemy, for "Who can forgive sins but God alone?" (Mark 2:7). Of course, they were absolutely correct with their accusation. Such was Torah; no one had this ability unless someone greater than Torah was present. Jesus's public exorcisms not only set the captives free, but revealed the kingdom of God had come to the people (Matt 12:28; Luke 11:20). While in prison, the Baptist asked Jesus if he was the expected Messiah. Response came in the form of a report of the message preached and the signs and wonders performed (Luke 7:18–23). Jesus submitted significant and substantial evidence for Israel to examine through the lens of the Law, Prophets, and Writings. Israel was forced to decide about Jesus. Some thought he was the Baptist, Elijah, Jeremiah, or another prophet. The only correct answer was "You are the Christ" (Matt 16:14–16).

Many throughout Israel acknowledged Jesus as Messiah and entered into the new covenant community, but most did not (Matt 7:13–14; 27:22). The disciples numbered 120 in Jerusalem on the day of Pentecost (Acts 1:15). In no way did Jesus's mission fail to accomplish its purpose. The prophets never described a time in which every Israelite would be spared from God's judgment. In fact, they declared that while a righteous remnant of the people of God would exist, many Jews would experience the same judgment as the unrighteous gentiles (Mal 3:5, 16–4:3).

## BLESSING THE NATIONS THROUGH JUDGMENT: A NEW COVENANT BY DEATH AND RESURRECTION

The Prophets speak of a covenant to come that would be everlasting and one of peace. Only once in the Old Testament is the adjective "new" used to describe this covenant, and that by Jeremiah.[19] From the prophets' perspectives, the new covenant is *new* because both God and his people would be

---

19. References to this new covenant may be found in Isaiah 54:1–10; 55:1–5; 61:8–9; Jeremiah 31:31–34; 32:36–41; 50:2–5; and Ezekiel 11:18–21; 18:30–32; 36:24–32; 34:20–31; 37:15–28.

able to keep it. Torah would be written on his people's hearts, and his Spirit would be placed within them as a result of the work of the eternal Davidic king (cf. 2 Sam 7). The "faulty" religious mediators Israel had known that led to divine wrath upon the nation would be no more. God would create a new covenant community characterized by its forgiven status.[20] This Son of David would bring a dynasty that would restore the dominion lost by Adam. His reign over God's people would not be limited to the Jewish people in Jerusalem but would encompass all nations over the entire world. His coming with a message of hope through judgment would result in a multiethnic multitude of God's image-bearers entering into relationship and the blessing of their Creator. The glorification of God throughout the world that was lost in Adam would be fulfilled in Christ.

The night before the crucifixion, Jesus establishes the new covenant with his disciples who gathered to observe Passover (Matt 26:26–29; Mark 14:22–25; Luke 22:14–23). The moment of the Lord's Supper is filled with Old Testament imagery and foreshadows events to come.[21] It represents reflection, redemption (Luke 22:19–20), and restoration (Matt 26:29; Mark 14:25; Luke 22:16). While the covenant blood is a different concept from Passover blood, creating a fusion of ideas, the theological truth of deliverance and redemption is present and profound.[22] Matthew notes it is Christ's blood that is "poured out for many for the forgiveness of sins" (Matt 26:28). For Mark, in particular, the cross becomes a focal point noting that blessing comes through judgment. Jesus's sacrifice would make possible the new expression of God's people.[23]

It would be this eschatological community that ushers in the kingdom of God. Their redemption would be much more than an individualistic salvation. Their submission to the Davidic Servant-King would empower

---

20. Peter J. Gentry and Stephen J. Wellum, *Kingdom through Covenant: A Biblical-Theological Understanding of the Covenants*, 2nd ed. (Wheaton, IL: Crossway, 2018), 555.

21. When examined from John's perspective, this evening comes with even greater clarity. Jesus was the lamb of God (John 1:29) and had been teaching about eating his flesh and drinking his blood (John 6:60–61, 66).

22. R. Alan Cole, *Mark: An Introduction and Commentary* (Grand Rapids: Eerdmans, 1961), 216.

23. Craig Blomberg writes: "The covenant language implies the creation of a community, now to be constituted of those who in their eating and drinking identify with the benefits of Jesus' sacrificial death. This 'true Israel' stands over against the natural Israel of the old covenant." *Matthew* (Nashville: Broadman & Holman, 1992), 391.

them for worship, witness, and service to a world quickly approaching the day of the Lord. In one sense, the kingdom arrived and they were to reflect life in that kingdom. In another sense, they had work to accomplish while they awaited the kingdom to come. The crucifixion and resurrection would have implications on the individual, the community of God's covenant people, and the created order.

The sacrificed-resurrected king inaugurates the new covenant and reveals the new life, both present and future. A day would arrive when the banquet table would be set for his people and he would drink the cup with them once again. Until that day, the mission of God is to continue to transform the nations. Kingdom citizens are "the vanguard of God's end-time messianic people committed to joining Jesus in his gathering mission."[24]

## BLESSING THE NATIONS THROUGH A PEOPLE: THE CHURCH TO REFLECT THE KINGDOM

Mark introduces Jesus's first words as "The time is fulfilled, and the kingdom of God is at hand; repent and believe in the gospel" (Mark 1:15; Matt 4:17). His message of turning from sin was characteristic of and in continuity with the prophets. Everything the Old Testament pointed toward regarding the coming kingdom was imminent. The blessings and judgment of God were about to occur. Yet Israel (Luke 17:20), including Jesus's disciples (Acts 1:6), would misunderstand both the timing of the events and how they would manifest themselves. Jesus's kingdom would eventually arrive in visible triumph (Matt 6:10), but prior to that moment, the kingdom of God would not be externally visible but in the midst of God's people (Luke 17:20–21).[25]

The prophets note when the kingdom comes, the gentiles would be gathered to the people of God. The time between Jesus's first and second coming is a period in which the kingdom of God is present to a degree but not yet fully manifested. As Isaiah, Jeremiah, and Ezekiel foretold, Israel would be restored and the gentiles would be ingathered. However, the New Testament writers reveal a mystery and clarification to the mission

---

24. Goheen, *A Light to the Nations*, 86.
25. Cole, *Mark*, 60.

of God described in the Old Testament. The people of God are not to be defined along ethnic, national, or geographical lines, but rather by faith that leads to righteous actions. God's family is understood as those who do the will of the Father (Matt 12:46–50). As the Davidic king and Suffering Servant, Jesus came to restore Israel under his reign and prepare her to serve as a blessing and light to the nations so they would stream to him and into his kingdom.[26] His message and ministry became the impetus for his people's mission.[27]

Jesus and the first century believers did not view themselves as the creators of a new religion. They recognized themselves to be a continuation of God's people and mission described throughout the Old Testament. Jesus's promise to build his church (Matt 16:18) was not a declaration of a new entity that would be a breakaway from Israel. The true people of God did not become a reality in the first century. They existed throughout the Old Testament alongside the unrighteous as they resided side-by-side in Israel.[28] The community under the king had been in existence. Jesus revealed God's people would be the *ekklesia* (church) made up of men and women from *panta ta ethne* (all the nations) while existing as the children of Abraham (cf. Gal 3:7–9).

The church is not the kingdom of God, but it exists under his rule and in submission to his reign (Luke 14:25–33). The ethic of the kingdom transcends the popular understanding of the Law (Matt 5:21–48). This way of life informs the disciples how they were to relate to God (Matt 22:34–38), other kingdom citizens (Matt 18:15–20), and those outside of the kingdom (Matt 22:39; 28:19–20).[29] The church is sent out and put on display before the watching world. What once should have been said by Israel to the nations now was to be proclaimed by the church: "Look at us, if you want to see

---

26. Goheen, *A Light to the Nations*, 76.

27. Donald Senior and Carroll Stuhlmueller, *The Biblical Foundations for Mission* (Maryknoll, NY: Orbis Books, 1983), 141.

28. Senior and Stuhlmueller, *The Biblical Foundations for Mission*, 84.

29. Paul G. Hiebert notes that "The Kingdom points us to the church. Here the King is worshiped, and here he delights to dwell. The church is the manifestation, however imperfect, of the Kingdom. It is to be a living example to the world of a covenant community of reconciliation that breaks down the human hostilities between races, classes, and genders. It is to be a servant community in which all care for one another." "Evangelism, Church, and Kingdom," in *The Good News of the Kingdom: Mission Theology for the Third Millennium*, ed. Charles Van Engen, Dean S. Gilliland, and Paul Pierson (Maryknoll, NY: Orbis Books, 1993), 160.

what the future holds! Become part of this community under the king's reign!"[30]

Consistent with the Old Testament view of judgment, the Gospels make it clear not everyone will enter into the kingdom (Matt 7:21; 25:41–46; Luke 13:22–30). Sown throughout the world are sons of the kingdom and sons of the evil one, with the latter to be thrown into the fiery furnace (Matt 13:36–43). People must hear and understand the word of the kingdom (Matt 13:19), repent, and receive it like a child (Mark 10:15). Then they will become part of the king's community.

## BLESSING THE NATIONS THROUGH A COMMAND: MAKE DISCIPLES OF JEWS AND GENTILES

Matthew and Luke draw early attention to Jesus's Abrahamic connection (Matt 1:1–17; Luke 3:23–38). The patriarch did not understand how the promise "in you all the families of the earth shall be blessed" (Gen 12:3) was to be fulfilled, but the Gospel writers bring some clarity to the matter. J. Richard Middleton notes the connection of the Abrahamic covenant, the Messiah's mission, and the post-Easter sending of the disciples:

> In the context of the overall biblical story, the Great Commission is best understood as a rearticulation of the Abrahamic calling, the vocation of the people of God to mediate blessing to all the nations of the world. In the New Testament, this vocation is understood as including the proclamation of the gospel, communicating the teaching of Jesus about the nature of the kingdom, and especially what God has done in the life, death, and resurrection of the Messiah. The result of this proclamation/teaching is that the band of originally Jewish disciples becomes greatly expanded as gentiles are added to their number.[31]

Jesus's last words to his disciples continues a two thousand year-old promise. They were about to engage with the Abrahamic covenant in a

---

30. Goheen writes, "The message of Israel's corporate life was to the 'this is where history is going—come and join us'" *A Light to the Nations*, 51.

31. J. Richard Middleton, *A New Heaven and a New Earth: Reclaiming Biblical Eschatology* (Grand Rapids: Baker Academic, 2014), 69.

way none of them could have conceived before the resurrection. Jesus's command is the basis for the gentile mission.[32]

This Great Commission is found in Matthew 28:18–20, Luke 24:46–49, John 20:21, and Acts 1:8. Mark foreshadows the global work in Mark 13:10 and 14:9.[33] A few important matters are worth noting regarding these passages. First, there is a comprehensive nature to what Jesus shares with the disciples. He has received *all* authority (possibly a reference to Dan 7:13–14). They are to go and make disciples of *all* nations, both Jews and gentiles.[34] Then they are to teach the nations to obey *all* of Jesus's commands (Matt 28:18–20).[35] Since Jesus will be with the disciples as they go (Matt 28:20), there will be no power to thwart his mission (cf. Matt 16:18). Once the Spirit comes upon them, they will receive a continual power for the task (Luke 24:49). Both Jew and gentile, of all nations, are eligible for citizenship in the kingdom of Christ.

Second, there is a specific message to be proclaimed to the nations. Forgiveness of sins and entrance into the kingdom was predicated on the Messiah's suffering and resurrection (Luke 24:46) and the human response of repentance (Luke 24:47) toward God. Those who receive this message become Christ's disciples, unite with his community, and follow his word that never passes away (Matt 24:35).

Third, the disciples are to bear witness to the Messiah beginning in Jerusalem. The predictions of the good news being preached throughout the whole world (Mark 13:10; 14:9) now begins to move from theory to reality. The centripetal approach to the nations coming to Jerusalem switches to a centrifugal operation moving away from Jerusalem.[36] Mark

---

32. Stephen G. Wilson, *The Gentiles and the Gentile Mission in Luke-Acts* (Cambridge, UK: Cambridge University Press, 1973), 243.

33. The disputed ending of Mark's Gospel (Mark 16:14–18) is considered by some his Great Commission account.

34. Schnabel notes that *panta ta ethne* may be interpreted as "all nations," including both Jews and gentiles, or excluding Jews and only referring to gentiles. He rightly notes that the context best fits with the inclusion of both groups. Schnabel, *Jesus and the Twelve*, 361.

35. It is beyond the scope of this book to address the great disputations surrounding the interpretation of the Matthean Great Commission. For details on the present views, see Eckhard J. Schnabel's discussion and numerous references in *Early Christian Mission: Jesus and the Twelve*, vol. 1 (Downers Grove, IL: InterVarsity Press, 2004), 348–67.

36. Eckhard J. Schnabel, *Early Christian Mission: Paul and the Early Church*, vol. 2 (Downers Grove, IL: InterVarsity Press, 2004), 1545.

couched his global vision in the context of the Judgment to come.[37] The post-Easter commissioning means the end is quickly approaching. The time has arrived for "universal proclamation and witness."[38] An urgency exists. The disciples must go *now*.

## CONCLUSION

God's mission in the Synoptics reaches its zenith with Jesus. Messiah arrives and establishes the new covenant. He is the servant, Davidic king, and Christ, who not only seeks and saves, but gives his life as a ransom for many (Mark 10:45; Matt 20:28). Bridging the epochs of the Old and New Testament, he comes to the Jews and spends the majority of his interactions with them. Gentiles are never turned away, but his teaching and ministry foreshadow the gentile mission that will occur post-Easter. He builds his church of the people of God and expects them to live in community with one another, according to his kingdom ethic in relation to God, other disciples, and those outside the kingdom. His gospel will be preached to all nations before the judgment.

## REFLECTION QUESTIONS

1.  Did you find it surprising that little attention is given to the gentiles in the Synoptics? If so, why?

2.  How do you interpret Jesus's response to the Syrophoenician woman (Mark 7:27) and commanding the Twelve to "go nowhere among the gentiles ... but go rather to the lost sheep of the house of Israel" (Matt 10:5–6)?

3.  What is the connection between the Abrahamic covenant (Gen 12:1–3) and the Great Commission (Matt 28:18–20)?

---

37. Joachim Jeremias writes, "with the death and resurrection of Jesus the eschatological hour has arrived. God no longer limits his saving grace to Israel, but turns in mercy to the whole gentile world." *Jesus' Promise to the Nations*, 39.

38. Senior and Stuhlmueller, *The Biblical Foundations for Mission*, 224.

# CHAPTER 7

# Mission in John

JOHN MAKES IT clear that mission begins with God and is intimately connected to his activities in the world.[1] He is the source from which all
missions extend.[2] The Word is revealed as Creator and the one who takes
on flesh to dwell among his image-bearers to bring them life and light into
their darkness (John 1:1-4, 9-14). God loves the world and sends his Son that
others may place faith in him for eternal life (John 3:16-17). John's eschatology
is a realized eschatology with a present and future perspective.[3] Those who
believe in him have everlasting life now; those who do not are already condemned though judgment day comes later (3:18, 5:29). Mission is related to the
covenant people bearing witness to what they have experienced regarding
God's gift so that others may come to experience the same gift.

Mission in the Fourth Gospel may be understood through the pattern of
purpose addressed in previous chapters.[4] One is sent into the world with

---

1. Köstenberger writes "the Fourth Gospel's focus is not on God's mission *per se*, but on his
mission *through Jesus* and on Jesus' mission through his followers." Andreas J. Köstenberger,
*The Missions of Jesus and the Disciples According to the Fourth Gospel* (Grand Rapids: Eerdmans,
1998), 41n53.

2. James McPolin, "Mission in the Fourth Gospel," in *The Irish Theological Quarterly* 36, no.
2 (April 1969), 114.

3. Teresa Okure, *The Johannine Approach to Mission: A Contextual Study of John 4:1-42*
(Tübingen: J. C. B. Mohr [Paul Siebeck], 1988), 167, 168.

4. Scholarship is divided over the view of mission in John's Gospel. For example, Ferdinand
Hahn advocates the Gospel has little to contribute to a proper understanding of mission though it
is not devoid of such attention (Hahn, *Mission in the New Testament*, 152). Harris, however, writes,
"It is John who provides us with the most developed theological understanding of mission and the
clearest outline of the abstract principles relating to mission" (Harris, *Mission in the Gospels*, 223).

a message of hope through judgment. Those who believe this message that Jesus is the Christ enter into relationship with him and receive the blessing of God equated with having life in his name (John 20:31). Those sent by God into the world to bear testimony to God and his Christ often experience suffering in conjunction with such kingdom labors. This chapter examines three aspects of mission in John: sending to the nations, sharing testimony with the nations, and suffering at the hands of the nations.

## BLESSING THE NATIONS THROUGH SENDING

The language of sending is used throughout the Fourth Gospel.[5] Sending occurs in the world, the location of all that is opposed to God and his goodness (1:10; 3:19; 7:7; 8:23; 12:25, 31; 14:17, 19, 30; 15:18–19; 16:11, 20, 33; 17:14, 25). The sent one in the ancient world both represented the sender's commission and authority. [6]Jesus explained this to his disciples after noting he was about to return to the Father for a period of time. While preparing a place for his followers, the Spirit would soon arrive to dwell within them (John 14:15–17), and they would be engaged in doing even greater works than what they observed in Jesus (John 14:12). Here the reader observes the connection of Jesus's death, resurrection, and ongoing mission. Jesus would be making a way for his disciples to the Father's house, (John 14:2), but such residence was not for them alone. He would reveal himself to the disciples through relationship; they would reveal him to the world (John 14:22) that others may enter into that same dwelling.

Relationship with God is critical in understanding mission in John's Gospel. Köstenberger assists here by summarizing John's principles of sending:

- The one sent is to bring glory and honor to the one who sent him.

- The one sent is not to do his own will but the will of the sender, to do his works and to speak his words, and to be accountable to the sender.

---

5. It should be noted that such language, while significant, is only one aspect of the language used by John to communicate mission. Okure, *The Johannine Approach to Mission*, 52–53.

6. Craig S. Keener, "Sent Like Jesus: Johannine Missiology (John 20:21–22)" in *Asian Journal of Pentecostal Studies* 12, no. 1 (2009), 23.

- The one sent is to represent the sender by bearing witness and exercising delegated authority.

- The one sent is to sustain an intimate relationship with the sender.[7]

These principles are observed in the pattern of purpose related to the sending of God's four particular representatives in the Gospel.[8] The Father sends John the Baptist to reveal the Christ. The Father sends the Son to provide eternal life. The Father and Son send the Spirit to comfort, convict, and empower for mission. The Son sends the disciples to bear witness to himself and the life he provides. As will be discussed, the sub-themes of testimony and suffering are closely related to John's understanding of mission. The human representatives sent by God provide a testimony to the relationship they have entered and blessings they have received but often experience suffering as a consequence of participating in God's mission.[9]

## JOHN THE BAPTIST

John introduces readers to John the Baptist. He is described as a forerunner to the Messiah. He was sent to Israel and came as a witness that all might believe (1:6–8). His ministry involved conducting baptisms, and through these acts God revealed the Christ (2:31–34). In the Synoptics, the Baptist is referred to as the Elijah who was to come before the Messiah (Mal 4:5; Matt 17:11). However, in John's Gospel he denies this label. Rather, when asked about his identity, the Baptist equates himself with the one Isaiah foretold who would be a voice crying out in the wilderness calling for people to prepare for the coming of the Lord (John 1:21–23; Isa 40:3).

Drawing from the sacrificial language of the Old Testament, the Baptist identifies Jesus as the "Lamb of God" who takes away the sins of the world (1:29, 36). Such shocking language not only personified the sacrifice, but extended the atonement beyond the borders of Israel! The Baptist's

---

7. Köstenberger, *The Missions of Jesus*, 108–11.

8. McPolin, "Mission in the Fourth Gospel," 113–14.

9. Testimony and suffering are not unique to John but may be found in the other Gospels and throughout many of the remaining books of the New Testament.

description encompassed something that was not possible even on the annual Day of Atonement.[10]

## JESUS

John views mission as a key theme in understanding the life and work of Jesus.[11] The church's mission builds off of Christ's mission.[12] John's prologue quickly identifies the subject of his Gospel. Drawing substantially from Old Testament language and imagery, the reader is reminded of Genesis's creation account in which God speaks everything into existence. The Word is this same Creator that was with God and was God (John 1:1). Beginning with the transcendent, John quickly moves to the immanent. The Word is sent from the Father into the world he created (John 3:17; 8:26; 10:36; 17:18, 21, 23) to glorify him and to do his will (John 7:28–29). He comes to bring light to darkness (John 1:5). This Creator takes on flesh and tabernacles among his people (John 1:14). He now expresses himself in a bodily form, unlike the cloud and fire that manifested themselves at the original tabernacle and led Israel through the wilderness. Moses foreshadowed his mission by elevating the serpent in the wilderness (John 3:14–15; 12:32).

Jesus comes to the Jews, but on the whole, they do not receive him (John 1:11). Isaiah predicted such would occur (John 12:36–43; cf. Isa 6:10; 53:1), though Jesus was quick to note salvation was from the Jews (John 4:22). He did not hide the fact that the Father sent him (John 8:42). He comes to obey the Father's commands so the world may know he loves the Father (John 14:31), and that the Father has shown his love to the world with the Son's arrival (John 3:16). As a Good Shepherd, he is sent to protect and care for the flock and bring in his "other sheep that are not of this fold" (John 10:16), possibly a reference beyond the Jews and Samaritans.[13] All

---

10. In the Passion narrative, John notes an even stronger connection between Jesus's sacrifice and the Old Testament. The Christ's bones were not broken on the cross (John 19:36–37) as a fulfillment of Exodus 12:46 and Numbers 9:12, passages referring to the Passover lamb.

11. Okure, *The Johannine Approach to Mission*, 36.

12. Wright, "The Bible and Christian Mission," 393.

13. Some scholars view the good shepherd narrative as a development of motifs in Ezekiel, Zechariah, and Isaiah. Jesus has come as the eschatological Shepherd-Teacher as opposed to the false shepherds. There is much merit to this conclusion, with the least being it reveals another point of continuity between the Messiah and the Old Testament. See Köstenberger, *The Missions of Jesus*, 133–38.

who received him, he gave the right to become the children of God (John 1:12). His coming was universal in scope. Whoever manifested faith in him would not perish but have eternal life (John 3:16). A day of judgment would arrive, for the disobedient were already under wrath (John 3:18, 36), but the initial sending of the Christ was not for judgment but salvation (John 3:17; 12:47).[14] Jesus would go to the cross for the sins of the world and would conquer death by resurrection. This blessing would be extended to his disciples, as he would raise them on the last day (John 6:35-40). His purpose involved bearing witness to the truth and accomplishing God's mission through himself (John 4:34).

The fourth chapter provides one of John's lengthy discourses, with significant insights to the mission of Jesus. The Evangelist notes Jesus had to pass through Samaria (4:4). His mission to the Samaritans offered another revelation that he is the Savior of the world (4:42).[15] In this text, Jesus describes the encounter to a harvest field. The disciples are told they are the reapers (John 4:36-38) collecting that for which others have labored. His sending from the Father is portrayed as unique, historic, and inaugurates the end-time mission addressed in the prophets.

John cites Zechariah 9:9 to show the fulfillment of the prophecy of the Messiah coming into Jerusalem on a young donkey (John 12:16). The crowds who heard of Jesus raising Lazarus came to meet him causing the Pharisees to note "the world has gone after him" (John 12:19). When taken in context, their statement has a great deal to say regarding the nations and the Messiah. Zechariah's context describes the arrival of the One who also speaks peace to the nations (Zech 9:10). While it is likely the Pharisees' world was a reference to the size of the Jewish crowd, John leverages this to show the universal aspect of the Messiah with the Greeks who sought to meet with Jesus (John 12:21). Jesus's words in this passage reveal the eschatological moment has arrived for his death that would bear much fruit (John 12:24). Widespread blessing would come, but it would come through

---

14. John's language shifts later in the book. Jesus soon notes, "For judgment I came into this world, that those who do not see may see, and those who see may become blind" (9:39).

15. Regarding this encounter, Okure writes, "the central thesis of the entire pericope is that Jesus is the sole eschatological and irreplaceable agent of God's gift of salvation who alone does and completes his work (vv. 10, 25-26, 34, 42)." Okure, *The Johannine Approach to Mission*, 182.

judgment.[16] Here Jesus states the ruler of this world will soon be destroyed, and then he will draw *all* people to himself (12:32). The warfare against the serpent was about to be waged with a crushing death blow to the head (Gen 3:15). It is from the "Jesus-shaped victory" that one finds the "root of the Jesus-focused mission of the church."[17] The floodgates were about to open. The gentiles would begin to stream into the kingdom, becoming children of God (John 1:12).

## TEMPLE

The narrative of the temple cleansing offers perspective into how John likely understood the relationship of Jesus to the temple. The money changers had transformed the place of worship and prayer into a place of business (John 2:16). John notes Jesus's violent expression is confirmation of what the Writings predicted concerning the Messiah's zeal for the temple (Ps 69:9). When the Jews confront Jesus over his actions by asking for a sign of his authority, his response is "destroy this temple, and in three days I will raise it up" (John 2:18–19). John offers the interpretation that "he was speaking about the temple of his body" (John 2:21). The Son of God who came to tabernacle among his people (John 1:14) was pointing to a much greater realty than a building void of the Spirit.[18]

There is much significance in this text concerning John's understanding of mission. More will be addressed regarding the temple and God's mission in the Pauline Epistles and Revelation. The implications found in this text, unless one is willing to accuse the Evangelist of allegory or simply making a comparison, is that the physical structure on Mount Zion is no longer significant (John 4:21–24). The temple is the Lord himself, and the Spirit that filled the original temple was about to fulfill prophecy and fill the Lord's disciples (John 14:17). Wherever they would go (John 20:21), the

---

16. F. F. Bruce, *The Gospel of John: Introduction, Exposition, and Notes* (Grand Rapids: Eerdmans, 1983), 264. Köstenberger notes that is it not clear as to whether or not these were Hellenistic Jews or gentile Greeks, and that John 12:24 may be a reference to reaching diaspora Jews and gentile proselytes. Köstenberger, *The Missions of Jesus*, 133.

17. Wright, "The Bible and Christian Mission," 391.

18. Whenever Jesus is present at the temple, it is not a stretch to conclude this is what Haggai foresaw when the Lord of hosts promised to fill Zerubbabel's temple with glory so that the later glory of his temple would be greater than what Solomon's temple had experienced (Hag 2:7–9).

Spirit would go with them. The nations would encounter the temple, but not necessarily in Jerusalem, and not as a physical building.[19]

## SPIRIT

The first introduction to the Spirit in the Fourth Gospel is in connection with the ministry of the Baptist. The Father sends the Spirit on the Son at his baptism. John notes that this act enables the Baptist to identify and bear witness to the Son, who will then baptize with the Spirit (John 1:29–34). After Jesus is glorified, the Spirit is given to believers (John 7:39). For John, entrance into the kingdom required being born of "water and the Spirit" (John 3:5). These images draw from Ezekiel's words regarding God cleansing his people. Though Israel had profaned God's reputation among the nations, he was going to act on behalf of his holy name and gather Israel from the nations, cleanse them with water, give them a new heart, and put his Spirit within them that they may obey him (Ezek 36:22–27; cf. John 20:22–23). It was likely the prophet's awesome dry-bones vision that John had in mind when he wrote these passages. The movement of the Spirit brought life and health to a hopeless, dried up people (Ezek 37:1–14). While elements of this prophecy were fulfilled with the return from Babylonian captivity, a greater fulfillment was to come. God's people would be unified, overseen by his servant David, under one shepherd, and walking in God's rules. And the result of such actions? The prophet declared, "Then the nations will know that I am the LORD who sanctifies Israel, when my sanctuary is in their midst forevermore" (Ezek 37:15–28). Being Abraham's descendants was insufficient for seeing the kingdom of God; a regeneration by the Spirit was necessary for life (John 6:63), and the Spirit would be provided without measure (John 3:34) that God's reputation would be known among the nations.

The Spirit is sent to be with the disciples forever. He is identified as another helper and Spirit of truth who comes to dwell with and in the disciples (John 14:15–17). The Son promises he and the Father will come

---

19. Beale's words, though beyond the scope of John's Gospel, are both clarifying and in line with mission in the book: "The task of the church in being God's temple, so filled with his presence, is to expand the temple of his presence and fill the earth with that glorious presence until God finally accomplishes this goal completely at the end of time. This is the church common, unified mission." *The Temple and the Church's Mission*, 648.

and make their home with the one who loves the Son. This indwelling is critical to mission in John. The Spirit empowers the disciples in fulfilling the task Christ has given them.[20] The Spirit is described as a Helper who is sent to teach and "bring to your remembrance all that I have said to you." And along with these matters, the disciples will receive God's peace (John 14:27). Such is needed, for they will be sent into a world loved by God, but one that hates them and the Son (John 15:18). They will experience persecution (John 15:20). However, the Spirit, sent from the Father and Son, will not only bear witness to the Messiah, but enable the disciples to bear witness to him as well (John 15:26–27).

The Spirit will arrive after the Son returns to the Father. This is to the disciples' advantage in the world. It is he that is sent to "convict the world concerning sin and righteousness and judgment" (John 16:7–11). As the disciples go, the Spirit will glorify the Son by revealing to them truth and important matters of the future (John 16:13–15).

## DISCIPLES

During the Samaritan discourse, Jesus tells his disciples that they are sent "to reap that for which you did not labor" (John 4:38). Later, Jesus acknowledges that he has sent the disciples as he has been sent by the Father (John 17:18). They were to bear witness to what they have seen, heard, and experienced (John 15:27) regarding the Messiah. Just as God had sent the Son *into* the world, Jesus desired his disciples to be in the world. Mission means engagement, not separation. D. A. Carson writes that Jesus's prayer reveals the continuation of what the Father had started:

> That Jesus' prayer for his disciples has as its end their mission to the world demonstrates that this Gospel is not introducing an absolute cleavage between Jesus' followers and the world. Not only were they drawn from the world (15:19), but the prayer that they may be kept safe in the world and sanctified by the truth so as to engage in mission to the world is ample evidence that they are the continuing locus of 3:16 'God so loved the world that he sent.'[21]

---

20. Hahn, *Mission in the New Testament*, 159.
21. D. A. Carson, *The Gospel According to John* (Grand Rapids: Eerdmans, 1991), 566–67.

Apart from Jesus, the disciples can do nothing of significance for the kingdom (John 15:2, 4–5). They are chosen to abide *exclusively* in him and, as branches, bear much fruit (John 15:8, 16) for God's glory. Intimacy was key to the continuation of mission. Jesus promised his disciples would do even greater works than he did. His prayer for "those who will believe in me" through the evangelistic labors of the disciples revealed the certainty of the mission continuing beyond the ascension (John 17:20).

Following the resurrection, Mary Magdalene was sent to the disciples to announce the resurrection (John 20:17–18). When Jesus first appeared to the disciples, he gave the Johannine Great Commission. He shared with them "as the Father has sent me, even so I am sending you" (John 20:21). Clearly, the disciples were unable to do some of the work exclusive to the second person of the Godhead. However, as his representatives, they were to take the good news, "it is finished," (John 19:30) into the world! The mission of the church is to proclaim this good news through the power of Christ.[22] The expectant promise of the Holy Spirit and the responsibility of proclamation are given by Jesus. Only the Lamb of God removes sins (John 1:29), but if his disciples do not preach the good news of forgiveness, then sins would not be forgiven (John 20:23).[23] Though the disciples are sent on mission into the same world as Jesus, their work adds nothing to Jesus's completed work.[24] They are the harvesters sent to reap in the field (John 4:38).[25]

## UNITY OF THE COMMUNITY

Mission for God's people has always been a communal effort. Solitary labors alone in the field were unheard of. The unity and community of the people of God have always been an important aspect of God's work in the world. The calling of Israel to be a "kingdom of priests and a holy nation" was more than just a function of a devout people (Exodus 19:6; cf. 1 Peter 2:9). It was a model to the world of the blessed life under the divine King. God's

---

22. Keener, "Sent Like Jesus," 45.

23. A detailed exegesis of this pericope is beyond the scope of this book. For an excellent treatment of this text and the different views related to the Spirit and forgiveness and retention of sins see Carson, *The Gospel According to John*, 646–56.

24. Köstenberger, *The Missions of Jesus*, 215.

25. Okure, *The Johannine Approach to Mission*, 200.

people were to be united around him and his Torah. Their community, lived according to his kingdom ethic, was to create a healthy jealousy among the nations, thereby driving them to this good King.

The expectation of unity and community continues in the New Testament. God's people find unity around him and his word and community with one another as they live together according to his ethic. The love of believers for one another was designed to point to Jesus. The new commandment that he gave for them to love one another was to be manifested to a watching world. It was through such interaction that all would know that they are his disciples (John 13:34–35). Love was not a new command. It was following Jesus's self-sacrificial model that the disciples were to manifest love toward one another (cf. 1 John 3:16).[26] Their unity would result in the world believing that the Father had sent the Son (17:20–21, 23). Their unity would serve as a powerful witness of the transforming power of the gospel and the fellowship that surrounds it.

## BLESSING THE NATIONS
## THROUGH TESTIMONY

Bearing witness to the Messiah is significant in John's understanding of mission. Such testimony comes from his disciples, but also from the signs performed (which are viewed as a testimony from the Father and Son). A testimony is shared so others may believe. In his prologue, John notes what he is describing is something he (and others) have seen (John 1:14). Many Samaritans believed in Jesus because of the Samaritan woman's testimony (John 4:39). Following the crucifixion, John notes that "He who saw it has borne witness—his testimony is true, and he knows that he is telling the truth—that you also may believe" (John 19:35). After the resurrection, he notes the signs of Jesus recorded in his gospel "are written so that you may believe that Jesus is the Christ, the Son of God, and that by believing you may have life in his name" (John 20:31). John concludes with a confession that he "is the disciple who is bearing witness about these things, and who has written these things, and we know that his testimony is true" (John 21:24).

---

26. Keener, "Sent Like Jesus," 44.

Jesus states both he and the Father bear witness about the Messiah (John 8:18). The works that Jesus does in the name of the Father bear witness to him (John 10:25; 14:11). He admonishes the Jews that even if they do not believe him, they should "believe the works, that you may know and understand that the Father is in me and I am in the Father" (John 10:38).

## BLESSING THE NATIONS THROUGH SUFFERING

The human agents of God sent into the world suffer persecution by the world. Though the Synoptics offer much detail about the arrest and death of the Baptist, John has very little to say other than a passing reference to his imprisonment (John 3:24; cf. Matt 14:1–12; Mark 6:17–29; Luke 3:19–20). Anyone who confessed Jesus as the Christ was put out of the synagogue (John 9:22, 12:42; 16:2). Though Jesus had overcome the world, the disciples would have tribulation as they engage in mission (John 16:33). They would be hated by the world because the world hated the Son (John 15:18–19) and because they were not of the kingdom of this world (John 17:14). Just as the Messiah suffered during his mission to bring life, in a similar way, his disciples would continue this suffering for the Messiah's mission.

Another reason for linking suffering to mission is that God's messengers bring an exclusive message of redemption to Jews and gentiles. Explicit faith in Jesus is necessary for salvation (John 14:6). Nicodemus, the teacher of Israel, (3:10) failed to understand that simply being a descendant of Abraham was not sufficient for eternal life. The Samaritan woman was told the Samaritans may have had their religious practices, but "you worship what you do not know" (4:22). Jesus's dialogue with the Jews revealed a devout group, but one that had misunderstood the God of Abraham and his plan and were equated as being slaves to sin and children of the devil (8:39–47, 54–59). Devotion to tradition is not sufficient for salvation, and speaking against such deeply held beliefs and practices often results in opposition.

## CONCLUSION

The Gospel of John has much to contribute to an understanding of God's mission. The signs of the Messiah point to something greater than themselves that others may believe Jesus is the Christ. Mission is primarily understood in terms of being *sent*. Though mission originates with God, John gives attention to those sent to participate in his work in the world. As the disciples go into the world, their unity and community will serve as a powerful testimony before a world intent on opposing their kingdom labors. Following the ascension, the work of the Spirit in the life of the community of disciples will greatly advance the kingdom among the nations.

## REFLECTION QUESTIONS

1. What is the significance of being *sent* in John's Gospel?

2. How does the love of the disciples for one another influence the way God's mission is carried out in the world?

3. Do you agree or disagree with the explanation given to the temple according to G. K. Beal in this chapter? Why?

# CHAPTER 8

# Mission in Acts

G OD'S GLORY THROUGH relationship and blessing continues throughout the book of Acts with the historical account of the advancement of the gospel and growth of the church. While this is most certainly one of the reasons for Luke's writing (Acts 1:1–5), he also had evangelistic, doctrinal, theological, and political motives as well. The book provides a continuity between the mission of God in the Old Testament and the New Testament. Luke provides an account of the kingdom's expansion grounded on the foundation established in Torah, Prophets, Writings, and his Gospel (Acts 1:1). The book begins with the expectation for the gospel to spread throughout Jerusalem (Acts 1:8) and concludes with its advancement throughout the ends of the earth without hindrance (Acts 28:31).

A great deal has been written on mission in the book of Acts. Given space limitations, this chapter will draw attention to the relationship between what was established in the Old Testament and continued in Acts. The apostolic work of the first century disciples was fueled by the belief that through Christ the eschaton entered history (Acts 2:14–36; 13:32–33; 1 Cor 15:14–15, 31–32, 45–57).[1] They experienced what the Prophets predicted and had a purpose to fulfill before the Lord's return.

It is beyond the scope of this introductory work to address the intricacies of the Lukan use of "proof from prophecy," as a literary device to explain or justify his points by referencing Old Testament passages. While scholars debate the extent of this mechanism in Luke-Acts, we cannot deny its

---

1. Okure, *The Johannine Approach to Mission*, 106.

existence.[2] Commenting on this matter to support the gentile mission in Luke-Acts, Stephen G. Wilson writes:

> The purpose of these frequent references is undoubtedly to legitimize both the original gentile mission and the subsequent gentile Churches, to show that this major turning point in the church's development was, from the beginning, part of the will of God. God did not have a sudden change of mind, nor was he caught unawares by an unexpected turn of events, for he had planned and willed it form the beginning. The gentile mission was not a novel element in the teaching of Jesus, nor did it occur simply as a result of the obduracy of the chosen people; its roots went back far deeper—to the eternal will of God. Of all the various methods Luke uses to justify the turning to the gentile, this appeal to the Old Testament and, by implication, to the eternal will of God, is the most profound and fundamental.[3]

Though the disciples misunderstood the timing of the consummation (Acts 1:6-7), including when the nations would stream to Jerusalem to serve the Messiah and God's people, Jesus reminded them the divine calendar was not in sync with theirs. The kingdom was to be restored, but not as they expected. The nations first had to receive the gospel. God's people were to be sent with the good news of hope through judgment. The Spirit would soon arrive (Acts 1:5, 8; cf. Luke 24:47) and following this end-time baptism, the disciples would bear witness to the life and work of the Messiah, in Jerusalem and throughout the world. Their acts would bring about a people of God the world had never seen.

Acts 1:8 serves as a rough outline of how the book unfolds. While the locations mark geographical boundaries of expansion from Jerusalem, the point of emphasis is more related to the gospel crossing cultural gaps. It is one thing for the Jerusalem disciples to share the good news with people like themselves, but God's mission does not end within one's culture and ethnic group. The church would soon engage the Samaritans (8:5),

---

2. Robert H. Stein, *Luke*, (Nashville: Broadman & Holman, 1992), 37.

3. Stephen G. Wilson, *Gentiles and the Gentile Mission in Luke-Acts* (Cambridge, UK: Cambridge University Press, 1973), 243-44.

God-fearers (8:27; 10), and gentiles (11:20). Just as the prophets foretold, God was about to gather his people from all nations. Acts provides the story of how the early Jewish disciples became part of a movement that would result in God's kingdom being filled with a multiethnic and multicultural population.

## BLESSING THE NATIONS
## THROUGH TRUE ISRAEL

Though little attention is given to Matthias or his selection, his addition to the Twelve is significant in God's plan. Judas's betrayal and suicide resulted in a vacancy among the original apostles whose number was reflective of the twelve tribes of Israel. Luke noted the Twelve would be in the kingdom, sit on thrones, and judge the tribes of Israel (Luke 22:28–30).[4] The destruction of Judas was foretold by David in Psalm 69:25 and the filling of his vacancy in Psalm 109:8 (cf. Acts 1:16–20). Joseph and Matthias were put forth as candidates who had been with the apostles and Jesus. Lots were cast and Matthias selected (Acts 1:21–26). The circle of the Twelve was now complete. The next significant event related to reaching the nations was about to occur.

## BLESSING THE NATIONS BY
## SENDING THE SPIRIT

The coming of the Spirit during Pentecost marked a significant date on God's eschatological calendar. This was the fulfillment of what had been promised to the people of God. The Spirit's filling was necessary for global witness (Acts 1:8), but his arrival also established a historical milepost on the way toward the restoration of all things.

Peter recognized and explained the details after the celebrants in Jerusalem expressed their perplexity regarding how they were able to hear

---

4. Commenting on the significance of returning the number of apostles to twelve, John B. Polhill observes the continuation of God's work among his people in the New Testament: "Their number corresponds to the tribes of Israel, for in a real sense they represent the restored Israel, the people of God. The continuity with Israel necessitates the restoration of the full number of twelve. Because the church is built on the foundation of these Twelve as representatives of the true Israel, the people of God of the messianic times, their number had to be completed before the coming of the Spirit and the "birth of the church." *Acts* (Nashville: Broadman & Holman, 1992), 93.

of God in their own languages (Acts 2:12). Peter noted this unusual matter was the fulfillment of Joel's prophecy (Acts 2:16–18; cf. Joel 2:28–32; Ezek 37:9–10). He applied the prophet's words to the last days and did not stop with an explanation of the situation but warned that, just as Joel stressed when this event occurred, the next thing to follow was God's judgment on the nations. Anyone who called upon the name of the Lord would be saved from this terrible day of destruction (Acts 2:19–22; cf. Rom 10:13).

The end had arrived.[5] The house of Israel had crucified the Messiah, now seated at the right hand of God (Acts 2:33). There was nowhere to run. The Messiah was about to make his enemies a footstool (Acts 2:35; cf. Ps 110:1). The Spirit came upon the people of God; judgment was to follow. The human response was to be repentance and baptism for the forgiveness of sins (Acts 2:38). Only then would one receive the gift of the Spirit, having been drawn into relationship with God (Acts 2:39). No longer would God only fill a few of his people for a limited duration of time. Now, the Spirit becomes a permanent eschatological marker of those who represent the new covenant community under the rule of the Davidic king.

## BLESSING THE NATIONS BY BEGINNING WITH THE JEWS

The response to Peter's message resulted in approximately three thousand baptisms followed by the converts' devotion to the apostles' teaching, fellowship, breaking of bread, prayer, sharing, praise, and evangelism (2:42–47). The last days had arrived. The church was established in Jerusalem and continued to increase in number.

At least five thousand people believed the apostles' words following the healing of the lame man at the Beautiful Gate (Acts 3:1–26; 4:4). Jesus's resurrection inaugurated a movement toward the new creation. Though the Jewish community put the Holy and Righteous One to death (according to prophecy), God raised him from the grave. The Messiah now remains in heaven "until the time for restoring all the things about which God spoke by the mouth of his holy prophets long ago" (Acts 3:21). Within this passage,

---

5. I. Howard Marshall, *The Acts of the Apostles: An Introduction and Commentary* (Grand Rapids: Eerdmans, 1980), 73.

Luke connects Jesus with the patriarchs, noting the blessing to Abraham comes first to the Jews, but then extends to the gentiles.

The Abrahamic covenant promised all the nations of the earth would be blessed (Acts 3:25; cf Gen 22:18). The Jews were the children of the prophets (3:25), and God had sent the Messiah to them for their salvation (3:26). Paul's testimony would agree with this passage that "nothing but what the prophets and Moses said would come to pass" (Acts 26:22). And what was their astounding prediction? According to Paul's testimony, "The Christ must suffer and that, by being the first to rise from the dead, he would proclaim light both to our people and to the gentiles" (Acts 26:19-23).[6] Though it took the disciples some time to understand the practical and theological implications of God's mission to the gentiles, the movement of the good news to the nations did not represent a shift in the development of the divine plan. The restoration of all things would not occur until Abraham's descendants first had the opportunity to receive the Messiah's good news and then the gentiles.

As the Jerusalem Church grew, both internal and external conflict arose (Acts 4:5-31; 5:1-11; 6:1-7). Following Stephen's martyrdom (Acts 7), Saul led a great persecution against the church (Acts 8:1-3). This opposition resulted in Philip taking the gospel to the Samaritans (Acts 8:4-5) and the Ethiopian eunuch (Acts 8:26-27). Though the disciples fled the city, the dispersion resulted in the gospel crossing new cultural barriers to reach the Samaritans, God-fearers, and gentiles. In an act of divine irony, the fleeing disciples eventually planted the church in Antioch from which a converted Saul would be sent to take the gospel to the nations (Acts 13:1-3). Opposition to the mission of God arose and hindered the expansion of the gospel in one area, but resulted in the multiplication of disciples and churches in another.

---

6. Wright notes in Acts "the *universality and particularity* of the Abrahamic covenant are now both embodied in Jesus of Nazareth. For he is the one through whom salvation is now available to *all* nations; but he is the *only* one to fill that role—not just for Israel but for all." *The Mission of God*, 515.

## BLESSING THE NATIONS BY PROVIDING
## A LIGHT FOR THE GENTILES

Chapter 13 marks a major turning point in the book of Acts. Paul becomes the main human character in the narrative, while Peter's representation diminishes. Luke is emphatic that the gentile mission in Acts was legitimate and not the result of a rogue band of disciples simply wanting to upset the status quo.[7]

Before considering Paul's significant declaration regarding the gentiles in Pisidia Antioch, it is important to observe his conversion. These narratives reveal evidence that the apostle never understood the gentile mission as secondary. His conversion is described three times in Acts with each emphasizing he would carry the gospel to the gentiles. The language used in Acts 26:15–18 is representative of the language used in the calling of Old Testament prophets (Ezek 2:1, 3; Jer 1:8). His commission is also described in terms similar to the servant passages of Isaiah 42:6–7 and 49:6.

Immediately following his encounter with Jesus, Paul is told he would be sent to the gentiles "to open their eyes, so that they may turn from darkness to light and from the power of Satan to God, that they may receive forgiveness of sins and a place among those who are sanctified by faith" (Acts 26:18). Ananias is informed that Paul would bear witness "before the gentiles and kings and the children of Israel" (Acts 9:15) and communicates this news to the apostle (Acts 22:15). While sharing his story with the crowd, Paul notes the Lord appeared to him in Jerusalem stating he would be sent "far away to the gentiles" (Acts 22:21).

Luke devotes significant space to the initial message spoken in Pisidia Antioch. It is here Paul's synagogue sermon traces God's mission throughout Israel's history, noting it was from the offspring of David, God "brought to Israel a Savior, Jesus, as he promised" (Acts 13:23). Though the people of Jerusalem had him crucified "because they did not recognize him nor understand the utterances of the prophets" (Acts 13:27), God raised him from the dead (Acts 13:30). The good news shared that day was that Jesus did not experience the corruption that followed death (Acts 13:35), is given the blessings of David (Acts 13:34; cf. Isa 55:3), and through him "forgiveness of sins is proclaimed to you, and by him everyone who believes is freed from

---

7. Wilson, *Gentiles and the Gentile Mission*, 241.

everything from which you could not be freed by the law of Moses" (Acts 13:38–39). Paul warns his audience not to be like the scoffers of Habakkuk's day who perished (13:41). While some believe and are urged to continue in the grace of God (Acts 13:43), by the following Sabbath, many Jews are filled with jealousy and begin to contradict Paul (13:45).

At this point in the narrative, it is revealed that Paul understands himself to be in line with the prophecy of Isaiah (Acts 13:47). Luke notes the gospel was to be spoken to the Jews first, but since they refused to receive it and considered themselves unworthy of eternal life (13:46), Paul and his team turn their attention toward the gentiles. The gentile mission was not the backup plan due to a negative receptivity on behalf of the Jews. The evangelization of the Hellenists in Antioch by unnamed men fleeing persecution by the hand of Saul (Acts 11:19–21) had foreshadowed much gospel proclamation throughout the gentile world by the mouth of Paul.

With knowledge of Paul's conversion in the background, how did he understand himself in connection with Isaiah? Luke notes the apostle also saw himself in one of the servant passages. Though the servant was to be a light to the gentiles (Isa 49:6), Paul understood this as a personal command for his team to follow: "The Lord has commanded us, saying, 'I have made you a light for the gentiles, that you may bring salvation to the ends of the earth'" (Acts 13:47). The hermeneutic expressed here is a noteworthy matter.[8] It would have been easy for Luke to apply the servant passage to Paul alone in view of the revelation that had been given to him. However, Luke connects the servant passage as a command to *both* Paul and Barnabas. What was inaugurated by Christ is appropriated by the church (i.e., the people of God).[9] Here is an important intersection of Christology and mission: Luke's use and application of the servant passage to disciples reveals a continuity between God's relationship to his people in the Old Testament and in the New Testament.[10]

---

8. For an extensive discussion of the various views of the use of Isa 49:6 in Acts 13:47 see James A. Meek, *The Gentile Mission in Old Testament Citations in Acts: Text, Hermeneutic, and Purpose* (London: T&T Clark, 2008), 43–54.

9. This is the language used by Meek when discussing the work of Richard Davidson (Meek, *The Gentile Mission*, 52).

10. Darrell L. Bock, "The Use of the Old Testament in Luke-Acts: Christology and Mission," in *Society of Biblical Literature Seminar Papers, 1990*, 29 (1990): 508.

Following Paul's Pisidia Antioch announcement of turning to the gentiles, Luke notes the gentiles began to glorify God, for "as many as were appointed to eternal life believed. And the word of the Lord was spreading throughout the whole region" (13:48–49). The first missionary journey would conclude with the team returning to Antioch to share "all that God had done with them, and how he had opened a door of faith the gentiles" (14:27). Though there was much celebration, there was also much conflict over the gentile mission. A boiling point would arrive that would almost lead to a split within the church. The first church council would take place in Jerusalem to address the matter.

## BLESSING THE NATIONS THROUGH A NEW MULTIETHNIC KINGDOM COMMUNITY

The gentiles' reception of the Holy Spirit and into the fellowship of the church was a highly controversial issue. It was one thing for the Samaritans to receive the Spirit (Acts 8:14–17), and it was controversial enough for the God-fearers to receive the Spirit (Acts 10:34–48). The Samaritans had historic connections with Israel and embraced elements of Torah.[11] God-fearers, while not proselytes, were devoted to much of Judaism.[12] However, the gentiles were of such a moral and cultural distance from the Jewish disciples that a radical shift had to occur in the minds and hearts of the apostles and elders. Peter had to experience a heavenly vision followed by an observance of the Holy Spirit's baptism of the household of Cornelius (Acts 10) to be convinced that the gentiles could be saved by faith. And even he was opposed by the circumcision party for allowing the mission of God to be an excuse for eating with the uncircumcised (Acts 11:3). Though matters related to the gentiles appeared to be settled following the Cornelius narrative (Acts 11:1–18), such was not the case. A contentious debate would manifest itself fully at the Jerusalem Council (Acts 15:1–21). Widespread

---

11. Marshall notes the Jews did not see the Samaritans as gentiles but "schismatics" in relation to Israel. See Marshall, *The Acts of the Apostles*, 153. Schnabel identifies the mission to the Samaritans as a mission to Israel. See Schnabel, *Paul and the Early Church*, 1071.

12. Marshall notes that God-fearers, particularly Cornelius, were not gentile proselytes, meaning they had not embraced all of Judaism, namely circumcision. While more liberal views may have prevailed in the diaspora, God-fearers were recognized as "pagans" by the Jewish communities throughout Palestine. See Marshall, *The Acts of the Apostles*, 183–84.

acceptance of uncircumcised gentiles as part of the church would come later, but not before Peter, Paul, Barnabas, and James addressed the matter.

In Jerusalem, Peter addresses the council and gives full support to the gentile mission. Not only does he share his experiences with the gentiles, but he acknowledges that God has cleansed their hearts by faith and makes no distinction between them and the Jews (Acts 15:8–9). Paul and Barnabas share their experience from the first journey (Acts 15:12). James has the final say in the matter, noting the prophets foretold the ingathering of the gentiles.

Drawing from Amos 9:11–12, James notes God promised to rebuild the tent of David, and even the gentiles would become part of the kingdom (Acts 15:16–17).[13] Since the Davidic Messiah had come and was now seated at the right hand of God, the dynasty had been restored. It was no surprise the gentiles should be under his reign; the prophesied time had come.[14] The language used in this text, "people for his name" (Acts 15:14) and "remnant" (Acts 15:17; cf. Amos 9:12), was applied historically to Israel. James's words (through Luke) reveal a profound theological depth related to who is now considered the people of God.[15]

The Council's conclusion was not to trouble the gentiles who turn to God, but to offer them a letter that would address a few points of significant tension between gentiles and Jews (Acts 15:19–21). In the eyes of God and the church, both Jews and gentiles were included as his redeemed people baptized with his Spirit. These relationships revealed the glory of God among all peoples. Their identity and unity in the Messiah and his ethic was to reflect a community that would bring the good news, through both words and actions, to the nations.

---

13. The tent or booth (Amos 9:11) is a reference to the house (i.e., eternal dynasty) promised in the Davidic Covenant (2 Sam 7:11). It is worth noting that Luke uses the Septuagint of the Amos passage, which some scholars have noted poses some interpretive challenges. For an extensive treatment on the language used in this pericope see Meek, *The Gentile Mission*, 56–94.

14. Meek, *The Gentile Mission*, 89.

15. Polhill states it well: "In the Gentiles, God was choosing a people for himself, a new restored people of God, Jew and Gentile in Christ, the true Israel. In the total message of Acts it is clear that the rebuilt house of David occurred in the Messiah. Christ was the scion of David who fulfilled the covenant of David and established a kingdom that would last forever (2 Sam 7:12f.); cf. Acts 13:32–34). From the beginning the Jewish Christians had realized that the promises to David were fulfilled in Christ. What they were now beginning to see, and what James saw foretold in Amos, was that these promises included the gentiles." *Acts* (Nashville: Broadman & Holman, 1992), 330.

## CONCLUSION

The book of Acts reveals how the story of God's glory through relationship and blessing continues, starting with the Jews and extending to the gentiles. God's sovereignty is observed through the fulfillment of numerous Old Testament prophecies in Acts. His mission to redeem and restore continues in the face of opposition. While the disciples experience threats, imprisonment, physical abuse, and death for their witness, the gospel continues to advance across cultural barriers.

The gospel is for both Jew and gentile. The good news of the Messiah's present reign and coming judgment and kingdom is a message to be communicated without discrimination. Overcoming internal and external challenges, the Spirit-filled church observes the multiplication of disciples, leaders, and churches throughout the world. The blessing of Abraham advances rapidly, resulting in a multiethnic community of kingdom citizens glorifying God through relationship as they await the full restoration of the kingdom.

## REFLECTION QUESTIONS

1. Were you aware of the significance of the Old Testament passages in relation to God's mission in Acts? If not, why not?

2. How should knowing that we are living in the last days affect the way we engage in God's mission both locally and globally?

3. What does it mean to be a "light to the gentiles"? Is it still possible for the church to do so today? If so, how?

# CHAPTER 9

# Mission in the Pauline Epistles

I T WAS IN the 1960s that biblical scholars began to turn their attentions in earnest to Paul's ministry and calling. Until that time, he was studied almost exclusively as a theologian; during that decade scholars came to recognize that Paul's theology was derived from his ministry experience.[1] Paul's theology developed from an amalgamation of sources. These were primarily his Old Testament convictions, conversion to Christ, the Spirit's special revelation of God's truth, and his ministry to Jews and gentiles. These areas converged and shaped his way of thinking about God and mission and are found throughout his writings.[2] This chapter examines a few of the significant subthemes of Paul's theology that relate to God's glory through relationship and blessing. Some of the questions addressed include: How did his conversion and calling influence his work? What was his view regarding the Messiah's relationship to both the Jews and gentiles? What was the relationship of Old Testament prophecy to how and where Paul carried out his apostolic labors? Was Paul only concerned about getting more people into the kingdom, or was church health also a priority? Did he expect the churches to carry on evangelistic work after he was gone?

Paul was Jewish, of the tribe of Benjamin, and a Pharisee (Phil 3:5; Rom 11:1). He was from Tarsus, educated by the reputable Gamaliel, and zealous for God (Acts 22:3). He had extensive training in Judaism and was hostile to

---

1. Bosch, *Transforming Mission*, 124.

2. I consider the thirteen Pauline Epistles of the New Testament to have been written by Paul, though the brevity of this chapter will not permit a thorough examination of his corpus.

the disciples of Jesus until his conversion (Acts 22:4). His understanding of the Hebrew Scriptures established a foundation on which he built his understanding of the Messiah and mission. Paul did not see himself as developing and propagating a new religion or a sect of Judaism. Rather, he believed his labors were a continuation of the mission of God in the Old Testament. His numerous references to Abraham, Israel's election, Moses and the Law, justification by faith, and mystery of the inclusion of the gentiles into God's kingdom provide continuity with God's original plan and purpose.[3] From Paul's perspective, God's redemptive and restorative plan had not changed. The fullness of time had arrived (Gal 4:4), Israel became partially hardened to the gospel, and the ingathering of the gentiles had begun (Rom 11:25). His relationship with Christ and apostolic calling moved him toward a new purpose in life and greatly influenced his apostolic imagination.

## BLESSING THE NATIONS THROUGH A MAN: PAUL'S CONVERSION AND CALLING

While Paul was not the only one making disciples and planting churches, he was significantly involved and influential in the church's first century labors, particularly among the gentiles. Hearing Jesus's question, "Why are you persecuting me?" (Acts 9:4) was sufficient to transform Paul's theological foundation and reorient his worldview. The one he opposed was the Righteous One from God who would soon bring judgment on the nations (2 Cor 5:10). The experience forced him to reexamine much of his views on the Old Testament. Paul's apostolic calling was related to his conversion. Though he was a persecutor of the church, God set him apart before his birth (Gal 1:15). As noted in the previous chapter, the language recalled God's words to Isaiah (Isa 49:5) and Jeremiah to be a prophet to the nations (Jer 1:5).[4]

---

3.  F. F. Bruce writes that Paul had the "conviction that he was a figure of eschatological significance, a key agent in the progress of salvation history, a chosen instrument in the Lord's hands to bring Gentiles into the obedience of faith as a necessary preparation for the ultimate salvation of all Israel and the consummation of God's redeeming purpose for the world." *Paul: Apostle of the Heart Set Free* (Grand Rapids: Eerdmans, 1977), 146.

4.  Arland J. Hultgren, "Paul's Christology and His Mission to the Gentiles," in Trevor J. Burke and Brian S. Rosener, eds., *Paul as Missionary: Identity, Activity, Theology, and Practice* (New York: T&T Clark, 2011), 116. Köstenberger and O'Brien note that some scholars have

Now, recognizing the true identity of the Messiah, Paul sought to persuade others to the faith (2 Cor 5:11). He wrote to the Galatians that following his conversion he was called to preach Christ among the gentiles (Gal 1:16; cf. 2:2,7–9).[5] Luke's account agrees with this testimony, but adds that Paul was to take the gospel to the Jews as well (Acts 9:15; 22:21), a group he never neglected (Rom 10:1). His salutation to the Romans notes the relationship of his calling and service among the gentiles:

> Paul, a servant of Christ Jesus, called to be an apostle, set apart for the gospel of God, which he promised beforehand through his prophets in the holy Scriptures, concerning his Son, who was descended from David according to the flesh and was declared to be the Son of God in power according to the Spirit of holiness by his resurrection from the dead, Jesus Christ our Lord, through whom we have received grace and apostleship to bring about the obedience of faith for the sake of his name among all the nations, including you who are called to belong to Jesus Christ. (Rom 1:1-6)

More will be said below regarding his calling to bring about the obedience of the gentiles.

## BLESSING THE NATIONS THROUGH A MESSAGE: JUSTIFICATION BY FAITH

Paul's understanding of the need for mission is deeply connected to the reality that neither Jew nor gentile are righteous, but all have turned aside from God's standards (Rom 3:10–12; cf. Pss 14:1–3; 53:1–3). Because of their status, God's wrath is upon them (Rom 1:18). Paul provides an extensive description of the state of people's sinful nature before God in the first three chapters of Romans. Everyone is dead in their trespasses (Eph 2:1). However, justification comes by faith and not through the works of the

---

shown doubts as to whether Paul draws from the language of Jeremiah (*Salvation to the Ends of the Earth*, 165).

5. Dean S. Gilliland states, "To speak of Paul's conversion as an experience that shaped basic convictions about his theology leads to the fact that coincident with his conversion he received the call to evangelize." *Pauline Theology and Mission Practice* (Grand Rapids: Baker Books, 1983), 29.

law (Rom 3:28; Gal 2:16). It is through relationship with the Creator that blessing is received.

Just as Abraham believed the word of God and was seen as righteous in God's eyes (Gen 15:6; Gal 3:6), both Jew and gentile had to follow this same path. For it was only through faith that people could become sons of Abraham (Gal 3:7). This necessary faith comes from hearing the word of Christ (Rom 10:17). Paul recognizes that the good news of the Messiah is the "power of God for salvation to everyone who believes, to the Jew first and also to the Greek" (Rom 1:16). While this message is "folly to those who are perishing," it is the power of God to those who are being saved by it (1 Cor 1:18). Paul proclaims this gospel that everyone may become righteous. According to him, Christ is the great equalizer:

> There is neither Jew nor Greek, there is neither slave nor free, there is no male and female, for you are all one in Christ Jesus. And if you are Christ's, then you are Abraham's offspring, heirs according to promise. (Gal 3:28–29)

Such sonship exists now outside of the confines of the Old Testament covenants.[6] Now through Christ, both Jews and gentiles, who were "alienated from the commonwealth of Israel and strangers to the covenants of promise," are built together into a holy temple for God (Eph 2:11–22). For Paul, the true children of Abraham (and thus recipients of the blessings of the Abrahamic covenant) are disciples of Jesus (Gal 3:7).

## BLESSING THE NATIONS THROUGH A MYSTERY: MERCY THROUGH RESISTANCE

Such acts of God among Jews and gentiles were considered a mystery in Christ, hidden for centuries (Rom 16:25; Eph 3:5). While Paul recognizes this historical reality, it is his understanding that the mystery is no more and is now a message to make clear to all (Col 4:3–4). It is revealed through Christ that all things in heaven and earth would be restored (Eph 1:9–10). Christ would be in his people, which includes the gentiles (Col 1:2). The

---

6. William J. Dumbrell, "Abraham and the Abrahamic Covenant in Galatians 3:1–14," in *The Gospel to the Nations: Perspectives on Paul's Mission*, eds. Peter Bolt and Mark Thompson (Downers Grove, IL: InterVarsity Press, 2000), 27.

mystery of the incorporation of both Jew and gentile into the people of God involves a hardening of Israel to the gospel. Because of disobedience, the branches of Jewish unbelievers were broken off the olive tree in order that the faithful wild olive shoot gentiles could be grafted in among the branches (Rom 11:17). Paul also notes this is a mystery worthy of understanding. Israel's resistance to the Messiah is temporary and remains "until the fullness of the gentiles has come in" (Rom 11:25). Ironically, this eschatological ingathering of the nations is a means of stirring up righteous jealousy among Israel so that the natural branches will be grafted in and the Jews come to salvation (Rom 11:11, 24, 26). While Paul did not view his ministry to the gentiles as simply a means to Israel's salvation, he understands the mercy shown to the gentiles as part of the mission of God to show mercy to the Jews (Rom 11:27, 31; cf. Isa 59:20, 21).

## BLESSING THE NATIONS THROUGH A PEOPLE: THE CHURCH

Paul recognizes a significant connection between his ministry and part of the servant's ministry in Isaiah. As noted in chapter eight, Luke records a connection between Paul's calling and ministry at Pisidia Antioch to Isaiah's servant. After the Jews resist the gospel in the city, Paul declares he and Barnabas are turning their attentions toward the gentiles. While Paul prefers to preach to receptive peoples, this strategic transition is not based on pragmatism. Rather, Luke notes the Lord gave them a command to take the good news to the gentiles. Where did Paul find such a command? According to Luke, it was from Isaiah: "I have made you a light for the gentiles, that you may bring salvation to the ends of the earth" (Acts 13:47).

Paul's use of Isaiah's servant passages raises questions. Did Paul see himself as the servant? Did he see the servant as the New Israel and that he was part of the New Israel? Or did Paul see Jesus as the servant, and because he was in Christ he was an extension of the servant?

Paul recognizes that Isaiah's Servant pointed to the Messiah. However, it appears his understanding is that the text relates not only to the Messiah, but also to the Messiah's church. While Jesus fulfills much of what was described in the Servant Songs, the servant's mission remains unfulfilled. The eschatological ingathering of the gentiles was yet to occur.

Though Paul draws from Isaiah, he is not claiming to be the servant. Instead, his labors come from and serve as a continuation of the servant's ministry.[7] Christ's resurrection empowers Paul to likewise take on the role of the servant in his gentile ministry.[8] This vision extends to Paul's understanding of the entire church, which cannot fulfill its God-given role without likewise becoming a servant.[9] While Jesus is the servant to bring about the restoration of Israel, the global reach to the nations was to follow the ascension. Paul apparently views the mission of the servant split between Jesus and the Church. The servant died and arose, but the good news was to extend to the ends of the earth through the church—in which Paul was a member. He is then able to personalize the servant's mission to the nations.[10]

### BLESSING THE NATIONS THROUGH A PLAN: PLANTING LOCAL KINGDOM COMMUNITIES

Paul was never a permanent attachment to the churches he planted. Rather, he maintained an itinerate ministry. He writes that his approach was to "to preach the gospel, not where Christ has already been named" as to avoid building on someone else's foundation (Rom 15:20). Paul's motivation for this method was not because he craved the novel. Rather, the apostle once again, roots his mission theology in the Prophets. Referencing Isaiah 52:15 ("Those who have never been told of him will see, and those who have never heard will understand"), his desire was to follow in Isaiah's servant's footsteps while advancing the gospel so that more people would come to faith (Rom 15:21).

After years of work, Paul concludes he "fulfilled the ministry of the gospel," forming an arc from Jerusalem to Illyricum (Rom 15:19).[11] He claims there is no longer "any room for work in these regions" (Rom 15:23). It is

---

7.  Köstenberger and O'Brien, *Salvation to the Ends of the Earth*, 166.

8.  Graeme Goldsworthy, "Biblical Theology and the Shape of Paul's Mission," in *The Gospel to the Nations: Perspectives on Paul's Mission*, ed. Peter Bolt and Mark Thompson (England: Apollos; Downers Grove, IL: InterVarsity Press, 2000), 14.

9.  Rowley, *The Missionary Message of the Old Testament*, 81.

10.  Christopher J. H. Wright, *The Mission of God: Unlocking the Bible's Grand Narrative* (Downer's Grove, IL: IVP Academic, 2006), 521. In no way does this diminish the language used at the time of Paul's conversion that draws from Isaiah's Servant. See chapter eight.

11.  For an extensive treatment of the intersection of Paul's mission and geography see Ksenija Magda, *Paul's Territoriality and Mission Strategy* (Tübingen, Germany: Mohr Siebeck, 2009).

now time for him to labor in new pioneer territory—Spain (Rom 15:24). What did Paul mean there was no place left for his labors? Did he think everyone had hear the gospel in this area? Regardless of the meaning, he was confident that it was time to depart.[12]

In the New Testament, church planting began with evangelism and resulted in new churches.[13] Rather than reorganizing long-term kingdom citizens from one church into a new one, the apostolic work started with disciple making among unbelievers. As people came to faith, they were gathered together into local expressions of the universal body of Christ. Following this, the apostolic task involved appointing elders over such kingdom communities (Acts 14:21-23; Titus 1:5). While others still needed to hear the gospel in areas from Jerusalem to Illyricum, the newly planted churches would continue to share the good news in their locales. As they lived out the kingdom ethic before unbelievers, they would have opportunities to display life under the Messiah's reign and share his message of hope through judgment.

After a church was planted, Paul and his teams would continue their apostolic work elsewhere. These transitions to pioneer areas were not to be understood as a lack of care for the new churches. Rather, the apostle who was excited the gospel was in the whole world and "bearing fruit and growing" (Col 1:5-6) and desired that this message would "speed ahead and be honored" (2 Thess 3:1), was the same apostle who desired to "present everyone mature in Christ" (Col 1:28) and "bring about the obedience of faith … among all the nations" (Rom 1:5; 16:26). It is a false dichotomy to think that Paul's understanding of mission was either about regeneration or sanctification. There was no dichotomy between the two. He was concerned with an increase of disciples and their growth in the faith.

---

12. Schnabel's comments are helpful here. He writes, "Paul either was convinced that [sic] had preached the gospel in Arabia, Syria, Cilicia, Cyprus, Galatia, Macedonia, Achaia and in province of Asia in such a manner as the nations needed to hear it before the Parousia (Mk 13:10), or he assumed that other missionaries and evangelists of the local congregations would carry the gospel to the cities and the thousands of villages that he had not visited." Schnabel, *Paul and the Early Church*, 1547.

13. See J. D. Payne, *Discovering Church Planting: An Introduction to the Whats, Whys, and Hows of Global Church Planting* (Downers Grove, IL: IVP Books, 2009) and J. D. Payne, *Apostolic Church Planting: Birthing New Churches from New Believers* (Downers Grove, IL: IVP Books, 2015).

The gospel was central for all of Paul's apostolic labors. He clearly preached the good news to unbelievers, but also writes to the Christians in Rome that he is "eager to preach the gospel to you also" (Rom 1:15), thus connecting the gospel to his teaching ministry too.[14] He understood his apostolic role involved evangelizing unbelievers for their salvation and teaching believers to obey the claims of Christ for their progress in sanctification. Therefore, at times when Paul wrote of the gospel, he applied it to *both* unbelievers *and* believers.[15]

Paul was also a "pastoral theologian,"[16] in which much of his epistles developed from his experiences. Even the contents of his prison writings reflect his ministry experience. The Pauline epistles are not theological treatises separated from disciple making. Paul considered himself a master builder (1 Cor 3:10). He would enter into a community, share the gospel, begin discipling the new believers as a local kingdom community, assist them with obtaining leaders, and travel elsewhere to repeat the process (Acts 14:21-23). The longest times on record of Paul in any given location, during his apostolic trips, are eighteen months in Corinth (Acts 18:11) and three years in Ephesus (Acts 20:31).

The Pastoral Epistles provide a glimpse of Paul's heart for newly planted churches. Titus was left on the island of Crete to "put what remained into order, and appoint elders in every town" (Titus 1:5).[17] Titus and Timothy receive guidance on the qualifications of elders (1 Tim 3:1-13; Titus 1:6-9). Timothy is instructed in the qualifications for deacons (1 Tim 3:8-13) and told to pass along sound teaching to others (2 Tim 2:2). In these three letters, Paul reveals his heart for the sanctification of the churches by offering

---

14. As P. T. O'Brien notes: "It needs therefore to be preached to those who have already received it and have become Christians. Believers do not leave the gospel behind or progress beyond it as they grow and mature in their faith. They stand fast in this kerygma and are being saved through it if they hold firmly to it (1 Cor 15:1-2), for it is in this authoritative announcement that true hope is held out to them (Col 1:5, 23)." *Gospel and Mission in the Writings of Paul: An Exegetical and Theological Analysis* (Grand Rapids: Baker Books, 1993), 63.

15. O'Brien, *Gospel and Mission in the Writings of Paul.*

16. Senior and Stuhlmueller, *The Biblical Foundations for Mission,* 178.

17. The appointing of elders soon after churches were planted also agrees with Luke's account (Acts 14:23).

encouragement, instruction, warnings, and exhortations to these two men who were to work with established churches and their elders.

## BLESSING THE NATIONS THROUGH A PROCESS: INGATHERING OF THE GENTILES

In the same context noted above where Paul makes plans to work in another territory, he references "the offering of the gentiles" (Rom 15:16).[18] This thought shows up in Isaiah, and given Paul's penchant for the prophet, it is no wonder some scholars see a connection. Some think the priestly activity of the "offering of the gentiles" in Romans 15:16 is connected to the prophet's vision of Isaiah 66. Others have advocated a link between Isaiah's words and Paul and the gentiles who traveled with him to bring the financial assistance to Jerusalem (1 Cor 16:1-4). If Paul understood himself to be part of fulfilling the mission of the servant during the last days, then it should be no surprise he uses Isaianic language reflecting this thought.

Paul seems to be combining Isaiah with the Old Testament perspective of the ingathering of the gentiles to Zion. If so, then he clarifies that the brothers from all the nations, who would serve as an offering are not the Jewish diaspora but gentiles.[19] Isaiah writes:

> For I know their works and their thoughts, and the time is coming to gather all nations and tongues. And they shall come and shall see my glory, and I will set a sign among them. And from them I will send survivors to the nations, to Tarshish, Pul, and Lud, who draw the bow, to Tubal and Javan, to the coastlands far away, that have not heard my fame or seen my glory. And they shall declare my glory among the nations. And they shall bring all your brothers from all the nations as an offering to the LORD. (Isa 66:18-20)

---

18. This is not a common expression for Paul. See Leon Morris, *The Epistle to the Romans*, (Grand Rapids; Eerdmans, 1988), 511.

19. Bosch, *Transforming Mission*, 146. Another perspective is that the "brothers from all the nations" are not gentiles, but Jews. However, this interpretation of regathering the Israelites does not seem to fit with the context and is definitely anticlimactic in view of verse 21 (Motyer, *Isaiah*, 459).

James M. Scott makes the argument that Paul has this passage in mind, which relates back to the Table of Nations in Genesis 10. Therefore, Paul's geographical movement from Jerusalem, as the center and starting point, to Illyricum (Rom 15) was connected to reaching the seventy (or seventy-two) nations from the Genesis list. According to Scott, as the apostle to the gentiles, Paul was primarily concerned with reaching the descendants of Noah's son Japheth, and his strategy was primarily geographical and not ethnically determined.[20]

While Scott has made a very important argument from a tradition-historical perspective, Schnabel believes his hypothesis founders "on account of the very diverse geographical identifications in the Jewish (and early Christian patristic) tradition, and also on account of the details of Paul's actual missionary work."[21] According to Schnabel, Paul's strategy was simple:

> He wanted to proclaim the message of Jesus Christ to Jews and gentiles in obedience to a divine commission, particularly in areas in which it had not been proclaimed before (Gal 2:7; Rom 15:14–21). The planning for the implementation of this goal likewise was relatively simple: he traveled on the major Roman roads and on smaller local roads from city to city, preaching the message of Jesus the Messiah and Savior and gathering new converts into local Christian communities. This is what he did in Arabia, in Syria, in Cilicia, on Cyprus, in the provinces of Galatia and Asia, in the provinces of Macedonia and Achaia, and presumably in Spain and on Crete.[22]

Regardless of the interpretation of the "offering of the gentiles," and the Table of Nations in the mind of Paul, what is clear is that the apostle

---

20. James M. Scott, *Paul and the Nations: The Old Testament and Jewish Background of Paul's Mission to the Nations with Special Reference to the Destination of Galatians* (Tübingen: J. C. B. Mohr [Paul Siebeck], 1995), 135–80. Bosch notes that Paul thought in terms of geographic regions and not ethnically. Paul "chooses cities that have a representative character. In each of these he lays the foundations for a Christian community, clearly in the hope that, from these strategic centers, the gospel will be carried into the surrounding countryside and towns" (Bosch, *Transforming Mission*, 130).

21. Schnabel, *Paul and the Early Church*, 1298. See pages 1298–99 for Schnabel's five counter points to Scott's argument.

22. Schnabel, *Paul and the Early Church*, 1299.

believed in the eschatological ingathering of the gentiles and that he was a participant in this divine process. The gentiles were included among the people of God through faith and not by works of the law. Abraham's act of faith and not that of circumcision was not only sufficient for salvation, but served as a model for all who followed (Gal 3:6–9).

Recalling the story of the patriarch, Paul writes that the Scriptures, knowing God would justify the gentiles in the same manner, shared the gospel with Abraham: "In you shall all the nations be blessed" (Gal 3:8; Gen 12:3). The Messiah would come in the fullness of time to redeem those under the law (Gal 4:4–5), but the blessing of Abraham would also come to the gentiles (Gal 3:14). Paul writes, "Christ became a servant to the circumcised to show God's truthfulness … to the patriarchs, and in order that the gentiles might glorify God for his mercy" (Rom 15:8–9).

The apostle references several Old Testament passages to explain to the Roman Christians that God has poured out his grace on the gentiles during the last days.

> For I tell you that Christ became a servant to the circumcised to show God's truthfulness, in order to confirm the promises given to the patriarchs, and in order that the gentiles might glorify God for his mercy. As it is written, "Therefore, I will praise you among the gentiles, and sing to your name" [2 Sam 22:50; Ps 18:49]. And again, it is said, "Rejoice, O gentiles, with his people" [Deut 32:43]. And again, "Praise the Lord, all you gentiles, and let all the peoples extol him" [Ps 117:1]. And again Isaiah says, "The root of Jesse will come, even he who arises to rule the gentiles; in him will the gentiles hope" [Isa 11:10]. (Rom 15:8–12)

If the eschatological ingathering had begun, then what did the future hold for Israel? Paul writes that a remnant in Israel would remain turned off to the gospel until the "fullness of the gentiles has come in" (Rom 11:25). The salvation of Israel occurs when Israel sees God's work among the gentiles.[23] This process of gentile ingathering would create a holy jealousy among Israel, resulting in the elect's salvation. The movement of the

---

23. Schnabel, *Paul and the Early Church*, 1319.

gentiles would be the means by which *both* the gentiles and Jews would come into relationship with God and under the reign of his Christ.

## BLESSING THE NATIONS THROUGH AN INVITATION: CALL TO THE LORD

The universal blessing of the gospel is noted in Paul's writings. He recognizes that "there is no distinction between Jew and Greek; for the same Lord is Lord of all" (Rom 10:12). However, though God desires his universal blessing to reach everyone, not everyone will believe (Rom 10:16; Isa 53:1). Referencing the same passage from Joel that Peter did on the day of Pentecost, Paul declares that "'Everyone who calls on the name of the Lord will be saved'" (Rom 10:13; cf. Joel 2:32). Yet, the nations will only be able to call on the Lord if someone is sent to them to extend the invitation (Rom 10:15; Isa 52:7; Nah 1:15).

## BLESSING THE NATIONS THROUGH A PEOPLE: GOD'S LIVING TEMPLE

Though Paul would visit the temple in Jerusalem to clarify a misconception (Acts 21:23–26), his language reveals a shift in understanding regarding the identity of the temple. Now that the Spirit has been poured out on all flesh (Joel 2:28 [3:1 in Hebrew]), Paul is able to write, "you are God's temple and that God's Spirit dwells in you. ... God's temple is holy, and you are that temple" (1 Cor 3:16–17).[24] Drawing from Leviticus, Paul also writes that God promised to walk among his people (Lev 26:12) as they kept themselves from ungodliness. As the temple had nothing to do with idols, the people of God were not to sever fellowship with him by becoming partners with unbelievers (2 Cor 6:14). Such action would bring defilement to the church and is to be avoided because his people "are the temple of the living God" (2 Cor 6:16).

In his letter to the Ephesians, Paul notes the church's unity. There is no separation between Jew and gentile in the kingdom. Jesus has removed the dividing wall to create one group from two through the cross. Echoing

---

24. This description of the temple follows Paul's warning that the day of judgment will test the works of the Church by divine fire. If the works prove to be righteous, a reward will be given. Such language is similar to Malachi's prophecy of the Lord coming to his temple, with a refiner's fire, to purify the priests (Mal 3:2–3).

Isaiah 57:19 where the Lord declares to the contrite healing and "peace, peace, to the far and to the near," Paul sees fulfillment in this Old Testament reference through Jesus who reconciled Jew and gentile to one another and brought the peace of God by preaching "peace to you who were far off and peace to those who were near" (Eph 2:17). Isaiah foretold of a time when the foreigner and the eunuch would "join themselves to the Lord" and that he would bring them to his holy mountain. They would join the Jews for worship at the temple—God's house of prayer for all peoples (Isa 56:1–8).[25]

For Paul, this prophecy finds fulfillment in Jesus, who established a foundation on which Jew and gentile grow together "into a holy temple in the Lord" (Eph 2:20–21). The growth of the church begins to fulfill the Old Testament vision of a restored temple.[26] The gathering of the nations occurs, but not to a physical building or nation.[27] The true temple is no longer on a hill in Jerusalem. The true temple is found where the community of believers is found. Instead of the predominate Old Testament centripetal understanding of the nations streaming to the temple in Jerusalem, the temple of God is sent to manifest itself among the peoples of the world. The nations still come to the temple, but not to a physical structure; rather to holy people making proclamation of peace. As both Jew and gentile enter into relationship with God, the temple will continue to grow until she fills the new earth (Rev 21–22).[28]

## BLESSING THE NATIONS THROUGH A PRACTICE: REGULAR AND INTENTIONAL EVANGELISM

Before concluding this chapter, a final contemporary issue needs to be addressed. Though Paul told Timothy to "do the work of an evangelist" (2 Tim 4:5), did Paul expect churches to engage in outward mission in their communities and beyond? Did Paul command his readers to evangelistic

---

25. Graeme Goldsworthy, "Biblical Theology and the Shape of Paul's Mission," *The Gospel to the Nations: Perspectives on Paul's Mission,* eds. Peter Bolt and Mark Thompson (Downers Grove, IL: InterVarsity Press, 2000), 17.

26. Beale, *The Temple and the Church's Mission,* 254.

27. Wright, *The Mission of God,* 524.

28. Again, as noted in chapter six, many scholars would disagree with this interpretation of the future temple.

labors? While we may be quick to say yes to both of these questions, upon examining the Scriptures, the answer is not as clear as most would like. Recent scholarship has not been silent on this issue either. James P. Ware argues that the reason Paul offers little exhortation to mission is because mission was assumed. The apostle did not need to tell them to do something they were already doing.[29] Paul Bowers says the answer to these questions is a resounding no.[30] According to Bowers, while Paul was evangelistic and sought the prayers and financial partnerships with churches for gospel advancement, he did not expect those churches to engage in their own apostolic labors. Rather, the churches, like Israel in the Old Testament, were to live such a lifestyle that the nations would be attracted to them. Paul practiced a centrifugal movement to mission, but the churches were to practice a centripetal movement.[31] As noted already in this book, churches are to have a centripetal element to their work, but Bowers fails to provide the full picture.

Robert L. Plummer has examined Paul's expectations in detail and offers helpful guidance. For Paul, it is the dynamic nature of the gospel that drives the churches to the nations. Unlike Luke, who gives a great deal of emphasis to the role of the Spirit in leading the church on mission, Paul gives attention to the inherent power of the gospel. Referencing 1 Corinthians 15:1–2, Plummer notes that the gospel in which believers stand is a sphere "in which the power of salvation is operative." Since the church now resides in this gospel, she "becomes an agent of its continuing advance."[32] The church of the Thessalonians was a prime example of a congregation that continued to carry the gospel beyond themselves with no recorded apostolic exhortation. Paul writes:

> And you became imitators of us and of the Lord, for you received
> the word in much affliction, with the joy of the Holy Spirit, so that
> you became an example to all the believers in Macedonia and in

29. James P. Ware, *Paul and the Mission of the Church: Philippians in Ancient Jewish Context* (Grand Rapids: Baker Academic, 2011), 235.

30. Paul Bowers, "Church and Mission in Paul," *Journal for the Study of the New Testament* 44 (1991): 89–111.

31. Bowers, "Church and Mission in Paul," 109.

32. Robert L. Plummer, *Paul's Understanding of the Church's Mission: Did the Apostle Paul Expect the Early Christian Communities to Evangelize?* (Eugene, OR: Wipf & Stock, 2006), 63–64.

Achaia. For not only has the word of the Lord sounded forth from you in Macedonia and Achaia, but your faith in God has gone forth everywhere, so that we need not say anything. (1 Thess 1:6–8)

After the gospel came to them (1 Thess 1:5), the new believers began to imitate the actions of the apostolic team. It should be noted that Paul also asked this church to pray for him, "that the word of the Lord may speed ahead and be honored, as happened among you" (2 Thess 3:1). Both of these texts note the active nature of the Word.

While it is true the Thessalonian example related to the church's faith before other churches, the sounding forth of the "word of the Lord" is clearly a reference to the gospel. In 1 Thessalonians 2, Paul notes that after they received the word of God they "became imitators of the churches of God," for they experienced persecution from gentiles, just as Paul (and others) did from the Jews who hindered him from "speaking to the gentiles that they might be saved" (1 Thess 2:13–16). They had suffered the same things as others (v. 14). In this context, it is safe to conclude that just as the apostle suffered for preaching the gospel, the church had suffered for following after his model.

In his letter to the Philippians, Paul reveals his excitement that others are preaching the gospel, and his command to the church is to follow in this fashion. Paul begins the letter reminding them of their "partnership in the gospel" (Phil 1:5). While this is a reference to a financial contribution (4:15–18), it is ultimately about their engaging with the apostle in kingdom advancement. Paul notes he has been imprisoned because of his labors. However, he rejoices because others have become emboldened to share the same gospel as a result of hearing of his circumstances. Paul's imprisonment has served to advance the gospel (Phil 1:12–14).

Contrary to Bowers, Ware sees within Philippians an explicit command for the church to engage in active mission. He makes a lengthy argument that Philippians 2:16 is best translated as "holding forth" the word of life and not "holding fast" to the word of life, as evidence for a missional command.[33] Ware concludes, "Philippians 2:16 reveals that Paul did not understand his apostolic mission as fulfilled in the establishment of

---

33. Ware, *Paul and the Mission of the Church*, 269–70.

firmly founded communities [Bowers], but in the independent spread of the gospel from the communities he founded."[34]

Paul concludes his letter to the Ephesians with the significant passage on spiritual warfare and the whole armor of God (Eph 6:1–20). In this text, his desire is for their prayers that he may boldly "proclaim the mystery of the gospel" (Eph 6:19–20; cf. Col 4:3–4). However, in their fight against the schemes of the devil, they are to put on, as shoes, "readiness given by the gospel of peace" (Eph 6:15). Such language draws from Isaiah's connection to the feet of the one who announces good news to Israel (Isa 52:7). This language could possibly be connected to Nahum 1:15. Regardless, the language is that of blessing and freedom to those who have been in captivity. In context, Paul's attention to the shoes of the gospel precedes his reference to taking up the "sword of the Spirit, which is the word of God" (Eph 6:17) and follow the text of the Messiah who came and "preached peace to you who were far off and peace to those who were near" (Eph 2:17). Clearly, believers are to be prepared to handle God's word appropriately which includes sharing it with regularity and intentionality.

One final passage to consider is related to 1 Corinthians 9–11. On different occasions Paul told others to follow his example (1 Cor 4:16; Phil 3:17; 4:9; 1 Thess 1:6; 2 Thess 3:9; 2 Tim 2:2). However, the context of 1 Corinthians 11:1 ("Be imitators of me, as I am of Christ") comes at the conclusion of Paul's discussions of his example and command to be a servant to others. He just addressed giving up one's rights regarding food so a weaker believer might not stumble in the faith (1 Cor 8:13) and giving up his own rights as an apostle so that he might win more Jews and gentiles (9:19). Paul was willing to surrender his rights if employing them meant an obstacle to the gospel would be erected before others (1 Cor 9:12). He would become "all things to all people, that by all means" he might save some (1 Cor 9:22). Just before exhorting the church to follow his example in 11:1, he concluded his section of the letter:

> So, whether you eat or drink, or whatever you do, do all to the glory of God. Give no offense to Jews or to Greeks or to the church of God, just as I try to please everyone in everything I do, not seeking my

---

34. Ware, *Paul and the Mission of the Church*, 284.

own advantage, but that of many, that they may be saved. Be imitators of me, as I am of Christ. (1 Cor 10:31–11:1)[35]

What Paul modeled before the churches was to continue with them after he was gone. They had received the good news; now that good news was not to end with them but intentionally be shared with others.

After reading the Pauline literature, one comes to a surprising conclusion: while there are important commands given to the churches for gospel proclamation to unbelievers, few such statements exist; they are largely assumed rather than stated directly.[36] The apostle offers little words on the subject that consumed his thinking and lifestyle. We must ask: why? Reflecting on this astounding reality, Plummer offers three reasons for the limitation. First, Paul writes to specific churches in unique contexts. The importance of his topics cannot be determined by the frequency or extent of how he addresses them. Second, Paul chooses to give attention to the advancement of the gospel from God's perspective. While human agency is an absolute necessity in such movement, it is de-emphasized. Finally, churches, such as the one in Thessalonica, were already involved in sharing the gospel. They did not need someone to tell them to start doing what they were already doing. Paul wrote to challenge them to display the kingdom ethic before the world.[37]

## CONCLUSION

The Pauline literature is a deep reservoir of information related to God's mission in the world.[38] This chapter has attempted to draw awareness to some of the most significant elements of Pauline theology related to God's mission.

---

35. Köstenberger and O'Brien note that "Paul is not suggesting that they should engage in the same wide-ranging, apostolic ministry in which he has been involved; but each *in his or her own way and according to their personal gifts* was to have the same orientation and ambitions as Paul himself, that is, of seeking by all possible means to save some." *Salvation to the Ends of the Earth*, 196.

36. Schnabel, *Paul and the Early Church*, 1456. Schnabel offers a summary and response to five reasons as to why Paul did not exhort local churches to engage in their own missional labors (1452–56).

37. Plummer, *Paul's Understanding of the Church's Mission*, 96.

38. We are very much in agreement with Bosch's sentiment: "Paul's thinking, truth to tell, is so complex that, at the end of a reflection like this, one has the distinct feeling of still standing only at the beginning." *Transforming Mission*, 170.

Yet, in this theological depth, Paul advocated a simple gospel that was a stumbling block to the Jews and foolishness to the gentiles (1 Cor 1:23). Everything changed for Paul when his relationship with Jesus began on the road to Damascus. Paul was convinced that salvation was extended by faith to Jew and gentile through Jesus who completed the messianic mission. But for before the application of such faith could happen, the church had to go to those who had never heard and proclaim the good news of a message of redemption and restoration that comes through judgment. Through Paul's preaching, kingdom communities were started in Roman provinces. As these local expressions of the body of Christ grew in the faith, they carried the gospel to others image-bearers in the world, bringing glory to God.

## REFLECTION QUESTIONS

1. In what way is your conversion to Christ like Paul's conversion? How is it different?

2. Is the call to follow Jesus also a call to engage in God's mission?

3. Is it possible to be more concerned about evangelism than church health? Is it possible to have healthy churches without those churches spreading the gospel?

4. Why was Paul willing to sacrifice so much for the advancement of the gospel?

# CHAPTER 10

# Mission in the General Epistles

AS THE GOSPEL continued to spread and the church grew, the young believers found themselves facing two significant challenges: tensions from within and opposition from without. Internal conflict resulted in strife and stress, hindering the fellowship of the saints. False teachers from among their ranks spread heretical doctrine and appealed to the fleshly passions of weaker members. As disciples multiplied, hostilities from the community and government increased. The Christian movement was birthed in a context of violence that continued throughout the first century.

The General Epistles were written in such environments. Their authors had much to say about these challenges. The church needed to know how to face opposition and suffering. Also, if the unity of the saints was hindered, false teachings embraced, and holiness compromised, then the mission of God would be interrupted in the world. If the churches failed to live according to the kingdom ethic in relation to God, one another, and those outside the kingdom, then the dissemination of the message of hope through judgment would not be taken to unbelievers. The nations would fail to hear the good news of the Davidic king and enter into the relationship that brings blessing. Some of the greatest hindrances to the advancement of the gospel are addressed in the General Epistles.

Few scholars have written on the topic of mission in the General Epistles. This is not a surprise given the aforementioned issues that demanded the church's attention. However, the language of mission is not absent from the General Epistles. Donald Senior notes that 1 Peter has much to say regarding mission, though he adds Hebrews, James, Jude, and 2 Peter have little to offer.[1] Köstenberger includes both 1 Peter and Hebrews as making important contributions to the theology of mission.[2] While I agree that little is stated in the General Epistles about mission in general, and in James, Jude, and 2 Peter in particular, these latter writings also have a contribution to make to a theology of mission. This chapter attempts to address the issues of how the churches were to live as witnesses and as kingdom citizens in the world through their suffering and lifestyles in view of the coming judgment.

## BLESSING THE NATIONS THROUGH STEADFASTNESS IN SUFFERING

The writer of Hebrews calls believers to remain faithful during difficulties and not to return to their former ways of Judaism. The mission of God to redeem humanity is retold throughout this book. God spoke through the prophets, and most importantly through his Son (Heb 1:1). It was the Son who was the sinless high priest (2:17; 4:15), offered the propitiation for sin (2:17), provided the eternal rest that no Old Testament saint was able to provide (4:3, 6), and completed his mission (12:1-2). Hebrews reveals the ultimate example of a mediator sent as an apostle into the world (3:1) to bear witness to God through suffering. The good news that he provided was that to which the church was to bear witness in the world. Just as the Son suffered as he engaged with God's mission, the church would likewise experience opposition as she lives as a kingdom citizen.

Hebrews notes the believers understood they were strangers and exiles in the fallen world waiting for the heavenly city (Heb 11; 13:14). The world in which they resided did not view them as friends, but at times saw them as objects to be persecuted.[3]

---

1. Senior and Stuhlmueller, *The Biblical Foundations for Mission*, 309.

2. Andreas J. Köstenberger, "Mission in the General Epistles," in *Mission in the New Testament: An Evangelical Approach*, ed. William J. Larkin Jr. and Joel F. Williams (Maryknoll, NY: Orbis Books, 1998), 189–206.

3. Reflecting on the recipients of this letter and their suffering for the gospel, Köstenberger and O'Brien write: "The book of Hebrews has no direct equivalent to Matthew's 'Great Commission.' But this does not mean that the epistle's author did not believe in the necessity of Christian outreach. Rather, it is assumed that believers' identity as followers, even disciples, of Christ will entail suffering which, in turn, will require the bearing of witness. While there are no clear lines of demarcation between verbal gospel proclamation and the

The general pattern of practice noted throughout this book (sending into the world → sharing the message → others entering into relationship → experiencing God's blessing) continues in the General Epistles. However, it is often around the sending and sharing stages that these letters give attention. As followers of Christ, the believers are sent into the world to live out the kingdom ethic in kingdom communities. Sometimes this practice brings persecution and suffering. Actions and words cannot be separated. Actions that show the gospel and words that share the gospel comprise every disciple's life. However, whether disciples are living in exile, scattered across great geographical distances or remaining in their locales, they are to bear witness to the Christ and his message through lifestyle and engagement with the world.

## BLESSING THE NATIONS
## THROUGH LIFESTYLE

James gives great importance to the practical results of the faith received. True faith produces godly actions in the life of the believer (2:14–26). Fifty commands are found in the 108 verses.[4] James writes to "the twelve tribes in the Dispersion" (1:1), Old Testament language that Jewish Christians, would understand. As the people of God, likely scattered due to persecution, they knew righteous living was important before a watching world. They had to be both hearers and doers of God's word (1:22). God's people were to reflect the faith they claimed to have received through God's mission in the world.

Senior and Stuhlmueller are quick to conclude that James has little to offer regarding mission. They note, "James urges the Christians to lead lives of integrity, translating their faith into active good deeds of justice and mutual respect. Although it could be inferred from the material, the author does not reflect explicitly on the witness value of such deeds."[5] While it is true that such a practical author does not exhort his readers to

---

witness of a godly life, … the two sustain an intricate relationship with each other." *Salvation to the Ends of the Earth*, 237.

4.   Walter A. Elwell and Robert W. Yarbrough, *Encountering the New Testament: A Historical and Theological Survey*, 3rd ed. (Grand Rapids: Baker Academic, 2013), 338.

5.   Senior and Stuhlmueller, *The Biblical Foundations for Mission*, 309.

make disciples, and preach the gospel, there is more to James on our topic than simply inferences.

James recognized that times of testing could easily throw his readers off balance and they could begin to stumble in faithfulness. He reminded them they should consider such struggles with joy and understand that the testing of their faith produces faithfulness (Jas 1:2–4). If they remain steadfast during their trials, they are guaranteed the crown of life (Jas 1:12). The prophets were an example of suffering and patience (Jas 5:10) and should be looked to as a model.

James comforts his readers by noting while the storms of life may rage and challenges to their faith may come, God dwells with his people (Jas 4:5), and he is compassionate and merciful (Jas 5:11). His mission brought them to life (Jas 1:18), a fact they must not forget living among unbelievers. The tension is evident between being in the world as God's people living out the kingdom ethic while not embracing the ethic of the age. Though they may be scattered in the world (Jas 1:1), they are not to become friends with the world. Such camaraderie is a sure way to end one's intimacy with God (Jas 4:4) and hinder witness.

John reminds his readers that the pull of the promises of this world is very strong, but the one who does the will of God abides forever (1 John 2:17). Eternal life is promised to them (1 John 2:25) and belongs to them (1 John 5:13). Since their sins have been forgiven, they have overcome the evil one (1 John 2:12–14) and the world (1 John 5:4). They are protected from the devil (1 John 5:18). This confidence is to encourage and empower them to righteous living and witness in a world that stands against the truth.

James tells his readers that since the mission of God brought the word to them that saves souls, then they are expected to put away wickedness (Jas 1:21). The word they received was able to bring transformation and designed to travel through them to others in need of the truth. They can avoid condemnation by avoiding swearing and speaking the truth (Jas 5:12). If someone has genuine faith, then his or her actions will be in line with the kingdom ethic. A person is justified before others when his or her faith produces works (Jas 2:14-26). Genuine faith cares for the needy and keeps the self from becoming stained by the world (Jas 1:27) and does not dishonor the poor (Jas 2:5). Such counter cultural actions of a kingdom citizen would have provided a powerful witness to the gospel in the first century.

God's people were to manifest lifestyles before the world that pointed to the king and his kingdom.

The light of God shining through his children into a dark world brings attention. Just as curious moths are drawn to a glowing streetlight on a summer's evening, John understood that the old commandment he was reminding his readers about (1 John 2:7) not only affected the community of saints, but revealed the nature of God to the world. If God is light (1 John 1:5), and the readers claim to walk in him but live in sin, they are liars before God and one another (1 John 1:6). To the outsider who does not know how followers of Jesus are supposed to act, such a lifestyle communicates falsehood and is contrary to the truth of the gospel.

God is love (1 John 4:8), and his followers are expected to love one another (1 John 2:10; 4:11). John recognized such was not only fundamental to proper fellowship and life in the church, but it would be by their love for one another that outsiders would recognize that they are followers of Jesus (cf. John 13:35). The love of the saints for one another is a powerful witness to the world that is passing away with all of its desires of the flesh, eyes, and pride of life (1 John 2:15–17).

John writes that his readers may not sin (1 John 2:1), but if they sin, Jesus is their advocate with the Father. His sacrifice appeased God's wrath against them (1 John 2:1–2). Part of God's mission toward John's readers involved John's care for them. He desired that his labors not be in vain. His readers were to make certain they did not lose what he had worked for in their lives (2 John 8). They were to confess their wrongdoings that fellowship may be restored with God and other believers (1 John 1:9).

James calls on his readers to find an example of suffering and patience in the lives of the prophets (Jas 5:10). These people of old manifested not only a faith that produced godly works, but also godly words. They were the ones "who spoke in the name of the Lord" (Jas 5:10). Such proclamation was directed to both the righteous and unrighteous. Unlike the false prophets, whose actions and language did not reflect the heart of God, the true prophets were on mission with God in the world.

James singles out Elijah as "a man with a nature like ours" (Jas 5:17) whose prayers withheld and brought rain upon the land. Though James's point is immediately related to the prayer of a righteous person (Jas 5:16), his readers would have understood the context. The wicked actions of

Israel and her leadership brought the judgment of drought. God, however, used his righteous servant as a witness of covenantal faithfulness to those who had gone after Baal and Asherah (1 Kings 16:29–34). Following the example of Elijah, James concludes by noting that "whoever brings back a sinner from his wandering will save his soul from death and will cover a multitude of sins" (Jas 5:19–20).

It is not a stretch to write that just as James believed true faith led to righteous living, he believed this lifestyle would include a continuation of the mission of God. Orthodoxy was to lead to godly practices, and such included the church's mission in the world. Old Testament saints who put their faith into action were not only a blessing to those around them, but manifested the glory of God to an unbelieving world. The first century believers were to do likewise.

## BLESSING THE NATIONS
## THROUGH ENGAGEMENT

Peter begins his letters with the language of election (1 Pet 1:1) and considers his readers coequals in the faith (2 Pet 1:1). God caused them to be born again and guarded for a salvation that is about to be fulfilled (1 Pet 1:3, 5). The apostle encourages them that though they find themselves grieved by fiery trials, the outcome of their faith is the salvation of their souls (1 Pet 1:9). They should take heart, knowing that Jesus also suffered for their salvation and was a part of God's mission that had been foretold by the prophets (1:10). When Jesus returns, he will bring grace to the readers, so they should prepare accordingly (1:13).

First Peter is concerned with the relationship between the church and the world.[6] Peter notes in addition to trials, temptations abound that attempt to conform believers to the passions of their former ways (1 Pet 1:14). Drawing from Leviticus, he reminds them that a call to be the people of the holy God is a call for them to be holy (1 Pet 1:16).[7] His readers are a significant part of God's mission in the world. God's plan to involve the Messiah was established long before the creation of the world, but revealed to them in the last days (1:20). This revelation is not simply a means to

---

6. Flemming, *Recovering the Full Mission of God*, 227.

7. Lev 11:44; 19:2.

increase their knowledge of theology. There are implications for action. Though life passes away, God's word remains forever (1 Pet 1:22–25). His promises and covenants do not change with the seasons, but remain constant. Such is the good news that they heard (1 Pet 1:25) and are expected to share with others.

Peter notes they are a unique and blessed people who have God's attention. His readers may feel insignificant as exiles in a troubling world, but they are far from that; figures throughout the Old Testament experienced similar exile status. They, like the church, were resident aliens and visiting strangers. Abraham was only able to bless the nations when he lived in this fashion among the nations. The same was true with Israel who was given a land that was not theirs but God's (Lev 25:23).[8]

The disciples are a chosen race and a holy nation (1 Pet 2:9). If this were not lofty enough, Peter includes their calling to God as a royal priesthood (1 Pet 2:5, 9). This language was used in Torah (Exod 19:6; Deut 7:6).[9] The new community of believers in Christ are no longer identified by their genetics or politics. Their identity transcends such characteristics.[10] Just as God elected his people in ancient days for his purpose of mission, Peter is applying this truth to his readers through Christ. Election does not provide recipients with the freedom to isolate from the rest of the world. Rather, it is a call to engagement. 1 Peter is a letter that helps balance identity in Christ with mission in the world, an exhortation to mission.[11] Living such a role in the world means they were to "proclaim the excellencies of him who called you out of darkness into his marvelous light" (1 Pet 2:9). They are God's people who have received his mercy and must live like it (1 Pet 2:10).

---

8. Moses Chin summarizes Peter's writing to the believers: "As the covenantal people of God they would find the life in transit one of difficulties and tension with the Gentile world at large, the State, their harsh employers, their unbelieving spouses, and even within themselves—an experience nothing less than a 'soul struggle' (2:11). Yet as the covenantal people of God, they were to declare the wonderful deeds of him who had redeemed them. They were to 'do good' in society so that through them 'the nations may bless themselves.' They should see themselves in continuity with the fulfilment of the Abrahamic covenant." "A Heavenly Home for the Homeless," *Tyndale Bulletin* 42, no. 1 (May 1991): 112.

9. P. J. Robinson, "Some Missiological Perspectives from 1 Peter 2:4–10," *Missionalia* 17, no. 3 (November 1989): 181.

10. Robinson, "Some Missiological Perspectives," 182.

11. Vladir R. Steuernagel, "An Exiled Community as a Missionary Community: A Study Based on 1 Peter 2:9, 10," *Evangelical Review of Theology* 40, no. 3 (2016): 201–2.

If they make known their election and calling by their actions, they will never fall and will receive entrance into the eternal kingdom (2 Pet 1:10-11).

Peter tells his readers they are to represent God before the world and to represent the world before God that others may be called out of darkness and receive mercy. The message of hope through judgment they were to share with their words and show with their lives was related to their identity as a chosen race, holy nation, and royal priesthood. Peter admonishes his readers to watch their conduct before the gentiles. Their actions represent the God they serve. His desire is that if they maintain an honorable lifestyle, unbelievers may one day glorify God when he returns (1 Pet 2:12). Jesus died that they may follow the way of righteousness in the dark world (1 Pet 2:24). Women, married to unbelieving men, are told to win over their husbands by their respectful and pure conduct (1 Pet 3:1-2). Everyone is to honor Christ as holy before a watching world and always be prepared "to make a defense to anyone who asks you for a reason for the hope that is in you" (1 Pet 3:15). In Jude's epistle, the author writes to exhort his readers to "contend for the faith that was once for all delivered to the saints," as ungodly people have crept in to the community of believers (Jude 3-4). The preservation of orthodoxy was, and remains, a necessity for the advancement of the gospel. There is no separation between right belief, righteous living, and kingdom advancement.

## WITNESS IN LIGHT OF THE COMING JUDGMENT

The culmination of salvation-history in the Messiah and the new covenant (Heb 8:6, 8-13; 9:15; 10:14-18) is addressed throughout the book of Hebrews while readers are warned both of a coming judgment (10:27, 29-31) and to avoid hardening their hearts and losing what they have received as a result of mission (3:8, 15; 4:7). The law was a shadow of things to come (10:1) and the righteous are those who have lived by faith as part of God's mission in the world.

The Judge is about to save and destroy (Jas 4:12). James's exhortation to righteous living is fueled by the fact that his readers belong to God and that God's judgment day is coming soon. Life is a vapor, only here for a moment and then vanishing. The foolish makes plans without considering the Lord's will (4:14). The rich have been unrighteous in their stewardship of their wealth and treatment of their workers. Their wicked actions have fattened themselves for the day of slaughter to come (5:1–6). While some of James's readers may have been the recipients of the actions of the rich, they were to remain patient with established hearts "for the coming of the Lord is at hand" (5:8). The knowledge that the Judge is standing at the door, was to keep them from grumbling against one another (5:9) and hindering the communion of the church.

Throughout the Old and New Testaments, false prophets and teachers are severely condemned. They not only make God to appear as a liar, but they lead multitudes of God's image-bearers away from entering into relationship with him and receiving his blessings. The General Epistles have much to state regarding such deception in the first century. False prophets would arise among the church. However, their condemnation and destruction are approaching (2 Pet 2:1, 3, 13). Jude offers strong words of warning to the false teachers and ungodly. "The gloom of utter darkness" has been reserved for them (Jude 13). The day of the Lord's visitation is coming (Jude 14–15), and Peter desires unbelievers to be prepared for that event (1 Pet 2:12). The Judge is ready to judge the living and the dead (1 Pet 4:5), for the end of all things is at hand (1 Pet 4:7). While there are warnings against the ungodly practices of the gentiles (1 Pet 4:3–6), elders are encouraged to shepherd well the disciples, for the Chief Shepherd will soon appear and reward them for their service (1 Pet 5:4). Believers are to keep themselves in God's love and wait for his mercy that leads to eternal life (Jude 21). Since they have already experienced this love and mercy, they are to have mercy on others (Jude 23). As they live out God's mission in the world, they must know the trials and temptations of life are unable to separate the people of God from his goodness. His power is so great that he is able to keep his people from stumbling and present them blameless on the day of judgment (Jude 24).

The last hour has arrived (1 John 2:18, 28) and John writes to offer some instructions before the Messiah was to return. He wants his readers to have confidence on the day of judgment (1 John 4:17) when they will become like him and see him as he is (1 John 3:2). The truth of God abides forever (2 John 2), but false teachers, though temporary, are a real threat to God's mission in and through the disciples. Believers were to test the spirits to discern those of God (1 John 4:1), for not every traveling teacher appearing to be engaged in God's mission is of the truth (2 John 10–11). Though Jesus came to destroy the works of the devil (1 John 3:8), the spirit of the anti-christ is alive and well on the earth (1 John 4:4). John draws attention to some traveling teachers who are continuing the mission of Christ. They are spreading the gospel and have love for the church. Such people are to be welcomed and supported, in contradiction to the actions of troublemak-ers such as Diotrephes (3 John 9–10). As the church shows hospitality and assistance to such apostolic laborers, they are considered "fellow workers for the truth" (3 John 8).

Some of the early disciples began to doubt Jesus's return. Such must have had an impact on their zeal to share the gospel. It had been several years since the ascension and still no sign of Jesus and the restoration of all things. People had died, and others were scoffing at this future reality. Peter notes that God's mission involves his patience. He does not operate on the same timetable as people's calendars. He is not constrained by time, and does not feel the effects of it (2 Pet 3:8). Rather, the appearance of his delay is a manifestation of his longsuffering in mission. He is "not wishing that any should perish, but that all should reach repentance" (2 Pet 3:9). Judgment will come for many, but God now extends the invitation to escape that dreaded day. And this invitation is extended to the world through his people. Could it be that part of the cause for the delay that brought dis-couragement was due to the church's neglect of God's mission?

The eschatology of 1 Peter lends itself to a missiological reading.[12] The future reality of judgment day and the destruction of the world are to govern the practices of the people of God. They are to live holy and godly lives that reflect their calling and be about hastening the day (2 Pet 3:11–12) through their sharing the gospel.

## CONCLUSION

The General Epistles offers a glimpse into some of the struggles of the early church. The authors were much concerned with the holiness and righteous living of the saints during their trials. Their walk with the Lord and fellow-ship with one another were critical to the global work to which they had

---

12. Dan O'Connor, "Holiness of Life as a Way of Christian Witness," *International Review of Mission* 80, no. 317 (Jan 1991): 23.

been called. Knowing that Jesus is coming and judgment day is near, the church must not shrink back from the gospel she received. Though these writings do not offer as extensive of a treatment on the topic of mission as some of the other New Testament writings, what is found here is a wealth of information on the subject.

### REFLECTION QUESTIONS

1. How does opposition and suffering hinder the spread of the gospel and the transformation of societies? Do they ever help spread the gospel?

2. What do you think Peter was doing when he described believers as a chosen race, holy nation, royal priesthood (1 Pet 2:5, 9)? How should these descriptors influence how the church should be engaged in God's mission today?

3. The General Epistles speak frequently about warnings against sin, false teachers, and judgment. How do warnings influence the advancement of God's mission in the world?

# CHAPTER 11

# Mission in Revelation

THE BOOK OF Revelation was written to the seven churches in Asia (Rev 1:4) and provides a glimpse into some of the contextual issues of the first century, as well as an unveiling of "the things that must soon take place" (Rev 1:1). John exhorts the churches to continued faithfulness.[1] The hermeneutical challenges related to this work should not keep the reader away. Rather, the one who hears and keeps the words of this prophecy is truly blessed (Rev 1:3). John writes the book to provide an eschatological continuity with the Old Testament.[2] This New Testament writing is rich in Old Testament imagery and serves as an excellent linchpin uniting mission theology of both testaments.

While the Old Testament saints clearly anticipated the age to come, it was the expanse of time bridging their present realities to this future that was less clear. The mission of God to redeem would continue until the day of the Lord. It was at that moment, separating the old age and the new age, that the eschaton would begin with the outpouring of the Spirit, ingathering of the nations, the Judgment, and the establishment of Messiah's restored eternal kingdom.

The New Testament clarifies and develops Old Testament eschatology. The mission of God continues with the coming of Christ who arrives to

---

1. Michael J. Gorman, *Reading Revelation Responsibly: Uncivil Worship and Witness: Following the Lamb into the New Creation* (Eugene, OR: Cascade Books, 2011), 176.

2. McNicol, *The Conversion of the Nations*, 104, 138.

give his life as a ransom for his people. He is resurrected and returns to heaven and sends the Spirit. His kingdom is inaugurated at advent, but comes in fullness when he returns. This *realized eschatology* has led some to argue for an overlap of the old and new ages until the parousia. The last days begin in the first century, and the pattern of purpose continues. The church is sent to bear witness to Christ and his kingdom, offering a foretaste of life in the kingdom to come. She is to proclaim a message of hope through judgment. The peoples who receive this message by faith enter into relationship with God and his people, and they experience his blessings. During these last days, the gentile ingathering takes place as the gospel advances. When Christ returns, the judgment and the new heaven and earth will follow.[3]

This chapter addresses six aspects of the Johannine perspective related to mission. John's observations and descriptions in this final book unite and develop several of the sub-themes already noted throughout the Scriptures. What began in Genesis (e.g., relationship, fall, redemption, promise) finds continuation and fulfillment in Revelation. The God who created his image-bearers to bring glory to himself throughout the world receives such glory from all nations.

## BLESSING THE NATIONS THROUGH PROMISES FULFILLED TO ABRAHAM AND DAVID

Most of the images used in Revelation are taken from Old Testament writings familiar to John's readers. Approximately 350 Old Testament allusions and references may be found in this book.[4] God is assumed as eternal and described as "the one who was and who is to come" (Rev 1:4). He is sovereign

---

3. Graeme Goldsworthy offers a helpful diagram portraying the Old Testament and New Testament perspectives, an idea he credits to Geerhardus Vos (Graeme Goldsworthy, *The Gospel in Revelation: Gospel and Apocalypse*, [Milton Keynes, UK: Paternoster, 1984], 71). It should also be noted there are differing perspectives on the eschatological realities to come particularly with matters regarding the millennium, Israel, and the church.

4. Elwell and Yarbrough, *Encountering the New Testament*, 358. David Mathewson shows extensive use of the Old Testament in just two chapters of Revelation (David Mathewson, *A New Heaven and a New Earth: The Meaning and Function of the Old Testament in Revelation 21:1–22:5* [New York: Sheffield Academic, 2003]).

over his people and the nations of earth. Both God and Jesus are described as being the Alpha and the Omega (Rev 1:8; 21:5–6; 22:13). Worship that is extended to God is also granted to Jesus (Rev 4:11; 5:12–13; 7:12). Jesus is the faithful witness to the things of God and the ruler of kings on earth (Rev 1:5). Jesus is the Lion of Judah and from the line of David (Rev 5:5) with the eternal dynasty (Rev 22:5; cf. 2 Sam 7). He is made to rule the nations with a rod of iron (Rev 12:5; 19:15) as King of kings and Lord of lords (Rev 19:16). John communicates the same One who created all things is worthy to receive worship from all nations. The promises of the Abrahamic and Davidic covenants come to fulfillment in this book as Christ's reign is universal and all of the nations are blessed.

## BLESSING THE NATIONS THROUGH THE LAMB'S RANSOM

Revelation notes that cosmic restoration and the universal reign of Christ came at great cost. Though John weeps loudly when he thinks no one is able to open the scroll of God to execute God's will in the cosmos (Rev 5:4), he is relieved to find "the Lion of the tribe of Judah, the Root of David, has conquered, so that he can open the scroll and its seven seals" (Rev 5:5). However, what John observes is an ironic sight of a "Lamb standing, as though it had been slain" (5:6) that prepares to unroll the scroll. It is at this moment the elders and living creatures around the throne worship the Lamb and provide insight into God's mission in the world:

> Worthy are you to take the scroll and to open its seals for you were slain, and by your blood you ransomed people for God from every tribe and language and people and nation, and you have made them a kingdom and priests to our God, and they shall reign on earth. (5:9–10)

These two verses reveal the centrality of the gospel, not only in Revelation, but in God's mission. The redemption of the fallen creation through the atoning sacrifice of Christ is the means by which God restores people to a right relationship with himself. This good news is available to all nations. The universality of the mission of God is shown in full. He has redeemed a multiethnic, multinational multitude of his image-bearers throughout history.

Jew and gentile are now united under one God and kingdom. They represent his priests on earth and "mediate their faith in him to others."[5] They also reign with him. This result is truly amazing. An ethnically diverse priesthood reigning with the Messiah would have been a scandalous thought. John draws from the language and concepts of Exodus 19:6 and Isaiah 61:6. Just as God gave the priesthood to his people at Sinai, the Lamb slain has the same authority to give such responsibility to the citizens of the kingdom (Rev 1:6).

## BLESSING THE NATIONS THROUGH SUFFERING AND DEATH

While the Lamb has provided the means to heal the nations and the cosmos, the message must be communicated to the nations and received by faith. The pattern of purpose continues through the church as she goes into the world, living out the kingdom ethic in word and actions that others may come to submit to her king.

Revelation notes the gospel continues to advance until the end in a world that is dominated by an ungodly system represented by the influence of Babylon. While the good news will advance throughout the nations, generally, societies will not progress for the better. Opposition to the church will come from both within and outside her ranks. False teachers destroy the testimony of the saints and mislead the world (Rev 2:2, 14, 20; 13:8, 14). Those who refuse to worship the image of the beast are slain (Rev 13:15). Without the support of the second beast, no one is able to buy or sell anything in the world (Rev 13:16–17). The two beasts are given authority over every tribe, people, language, and nation (Rev 13:7, 12). The nations of the world are in alignment with the great prostitute Babylon (Rev 17:2, 5). Though the nations of the world will make war with the Lamb of God, they will be destroyed (Rev 17:14; 19:21). Babylon will fall (Rev 18), but not before she wreaks great havoc on the saints of God.

In this context of violence, John observes and hears a startling reality under the altar in heaven. The souls of the martyrs cry out to God for vengeance, but are given glorious garments and told "to rest a little longer,

---

5. Morris Ashcraft, "Revelation," in *The Broadman Bible Commentary*, vol. 12 (Nashville: Broadman & Holman, 1972), 259.

until the number of their fellow servants and their brothers should be complete, who were to be killed as they themselves had been" (Rev 6:11). Those who conquered the beast and its image glorify God who worked his mission through their suffering (Rev 15:2).[6]

Faithful service in God's mission does not guarantee protection from such evil. As Jesus promised in the Gospels, it is a dangerous thing to follow him on mission in a world controlled by the god of this age. Faithfulness may result in exile (Rev 1:9) and prison (Rev 2:10). Satan is alive and well and described as dwelling in Pergamum (Rev 2:13), the same city in which one of the churches resides. The evil dragon makes war "on those who keep the commandments of God and hold to the testimony of Jesus" (Rev 12:17). The satanic beast is allowed to make war on the saints and conquer them (Rev 13:7).[7] Yet, in such opposition, John calls for believers to remain faithful and endure (Rev 13:10). They are to bear witness to the gospel and the coming kingdom that the nations may come to live under the king's reign. The faithful who perish during such acts are blessed (Rev 14:13).

The violent satanic opposition toward the church is fierce, yet the nations find blessing in Christ even when the disciples suffer for their witness. The faithful are the ones who conquer the devil "by the blood of the Lamb and by the word of their testimony" (Rev 12:11). While it may appear that satanic opposition has the upper hand, it is Jesus who holds control over Death and Hades (Rev 1:19) and eventually casts them, along with Satan and his demons, into the lake of fire (Rev 19:20; 20:10, 14). The seed of the woman crushed the head of the serpent on the cross and in the tomb. Soon that seed will cast the serpent into hell.

## BLESSING THE NATIONS THROUGH ENCOURAGEMENT AND EXHORTATION

Though the book concludes with the amazing defeat of death and the removal of suffering (Rev 21:4; cf. Isa 25:8), much of the book contains a dark shadow of hurt, death, opposition, war, famine, and judgment. Therefore,

---

6. Richard Bauckham, *The Climax of Prophecy: Studies on the Book of Revelation* (Edinburgh: T&T Clark, 1993), 306.

7. Some Greek manuscripts omit this statement from Revelation 13:7.

John begins by extending grace and peace from God to the churches (1:4) and reminds them of Jesus's love and sacrifice for their freedom from sin (Rev 1:5). He draws attention to the fact they have been made a kingdom of priests (Rev 1:6), and this Jesus is not only the firstborn of the dead, but is the ruler of kings on earth (Rev 1:5). It is brought to their attention that they are to continue representing the king before the nations and the nations before the king. Such use of priestly language representing the people of God reveals a continuity with that found in both the Old and New Testaments (Exod 19:6; Isa 61:6; 1 Pet 2:9).

From this reminder, Revelation unfolds with Jesus acknowledging the difficulties of the seven churches in Asia. Kingdom life and labors are challenging in a world that shows no respect for the king and his people. The king is in control, but matters are to get worse, much worse on the earth, before things get better. For this reason, John writes to emphasize God's sovereignty and from there provide encouragement and exhortation to faithful service. Jesus reminds the churches he is well aware of their endurance and faithfulness and that they should continue to walk in such practice (Rev 2:3, 19; 3:10). A day is coming when the kingdom of this world will become the kingdom of God and his Christ. And his kingdom will never end (Rev 11:15).

Revelation encourages mission.[8] Those bearing witness to the gospel frequently need encouragement, and John pauses at times to call the churches to endurance and faithfulness (Rev 13:10; 14:12; 16:15). It is the faithful who are rewarded by being spared from the second death (Rev 2:11). John writes to encourage and exhort the churches to continue in witness by visualizing a description of the throne room of God. The followers of Jesus have gone into the world to make disciples of all nations (Matt 28:19), and John's heavenly observation reveals the fruit of their labors.

John records the view of "a great multitude that no one could number, from every nation, from all tribes and peoples and languages, standing before the throne and before the Lamb" (Rev 7:9). Satanic persecution to the church has been fierce (Rev 2:10), but the gospel has been preached to all nations and a countless number have believed (cf. Isa 55:11; Matt 24:14).

---

8. Gorman, *Reading Revelation Responsibly*, 169.

The church's involvement in God's mission did not fail. Though they will have struggles and great challenges, God will accomplish his purposes in and through his people. The promises to Abraham find fulfillment and the nations rejoice and find rest in their God and his blessing.

## BLESSING THE NATIONS THROUGH THE RETURN OF THE KING

The book begins and ends with the notion that the tribulation, judgment, destruction of Satan, the parousia, and the manifestation of the new heaven and new earth are soon to occur. Even the devil knows his time is short (Rev 12:12). John calls his readers to attention, writing that what they are about to read (or hear) must soon take place and that the time for these cosmic events is near (Rev 1:1, 3). His salutation notes that Jesus is coming (Rev 1:7). Jesus's words to the church in Philadelphia are that even though a time of difficulty is coming upon the earth, they should hold fast to the faith, for he reminds them, "I am coming soon" (Rev 3:11).

In the latter half of the book, John describes the horrific results of the seven bowls of God's wrath that are poured out on the earth. Within this passage, a parenthetical statement is made that Jesus is about to return like a thief. However, the blessed one is the person ready for his arrival (Rev 16:15; cf. Matt 24:43; 1 Thess 5:1-4; 2 Pet 3:10).

The judgment of God comes at the proper time (Rev 14:6-7). God shows himself patiently desiring the repentance of the wicked (Rev 2:21-22). The breaking of each seal on the scroll brings about a different plague on earth, reminding the reader of God's judgment on Egypt that brought Israel from captivity and to the place of rest. Given time, the church would also experience deliverance from the evils of sin, Satan, and the ungodly world system. Many of the inhabitants of the world, like pharaoh, fail to repent of their sins (Rev 9:20-21; 16:11).

God's longsuffering expires. The climax of his judgments arrives. Condemnation falls on the devil, beast, false prophet (Rev 19:20; 20:10) and world. The countless opportunities for the peoples' repentance and submission to Christ have passed. The sins of the nations reach their full. Evangelistic work comes to an end. Neither life nor death keeps anyone away from this day. The dead are made to stand before the judgment seat. They are judged according to what they did in life (Rev 20:12). Those whose names are not in the book of life are cast into the lake of fire (Rev 20:15). Those who walk in repentance and faith have their names permanently written in this book (Rev 3:5; 21:27).

The final words of Revelation reiterate the emphasis on the king's return. The reader is reminded to keep the words of this book for Jesus is coming soon (Rev 22:7). John is told not to seal up the words of this revelation, because the time is near (Rev 22:10). When Jesus returns, he will bring recompense and repay everyone for their actions (Rev 22:12). And in case such redundancy is insufficient to communicate the point, "Surely I am coming soon" concludes the book before John extends grace to his readers (Rev 22:20).

Calling attention to the suddenness of the events of the book serves various purposes. Any believers who may be considering abandoning the faith or neglecting faithfulness should temper such thoughts with the king's return. When he arrives, he will bring his reward with him. The blessings promised to the nations will arrive, but the gospel must reach the nations while time remains. The intimacy of God's fellowship with his people will no longer be hindered by sin. The churches in the midst of trials and persecutions are to take courage and remain faithful in bearing witness to the gospel they have received. Christ has not forgotten them and is returning soon, and they must continue the global task before the end.

## BLESSING THE NATIONS THROUGH THE ELECT'S REDEMPTION AND COSMIC RESTORATION

The application of God's mission is universalistic. He desires to bless the nations through redemption in Christ. John's vision reveals this is not the same as universalism, the belief that everyone will be saved.[9] If John had not made this point clear with his vision of the great white throne judgment (Rev 20:11–15), he reiterates his point in a different fashion regarding the new Jerusalem: "nothing unclean will ever enter it, nor anyone who does what is detestable or false, but only those who are written in

---

9. For a brief description of the differing perspectives on universalism in Revelation see Mathewson's discussion (*A New Heaven and a New Earth*, 170–75).

the Lamb's book of life" (Rev 21:27).[10] The dogs, sorcerers, sexual immoral, murderers, idolaters, and "everyone who loves and practices falsehood" (Rev 22:15) are those who are not permitted in the city of God.

It is the followers of Christ who receive the blessing of the healing of the nations and experience the delight of the restoration of all things. They are the ones who conquer (Rev 2:7) and are faithful unto death (Rev 2:10; 12:11). They are from every tribe, language, people, and nation (Rev 5:9; 7:9). Their foreheads are marked with the seal of God and not with the mark of the beast (Rev 7:3–4; 13:16–18). They worship God and the Lamb (Rev 7:10). Their faith in Christ endures (Rev 13:10). They are the ones who keep God's commandments, their faith is in Jesus, and they die in the Lord (Rev 14:12–13). They are chosen by God, are faithful, and do not participate in the sins of Babylon (Rev 17:14; 18:4). Their names are written in the Lamb's book of life (Rev 17:8; 20:15; 21:27), and they are present at the marriage supper of the Lamb (Rev 19:7). They have the right to the tree of life (Rev 22:14) and drink of the water of life (Rev 22:17).

The biblical theme of restoration reaches its climax in Revelation. The reader finally encounters the scene where the one who tempted Adam and Eve is destroyed and a new heaven and earth are formed (cf. 2 Pet 3:13; Isa 65:17; 66:22). John notes, "The kingdom of the world has become the kingdom of our Lord and of his Christ, and he shall reign forever and ever" (Rev 11:15). This recreation reminds readers of a variation of Eden. God proclaims, "Behold, I am making all things new" (Rev 21:5) and announces "It is done!" (Rev 21:6) as the holy city descends from heaven as a bride prepared for a wedding. This place is for those who desire it and are conquerers (Rev 21:7), while those who practice sin find their portion in the lake of fire (Rev 21:8).

Missing from the new heaven and earth is the physical temple. However, the massive dimensions of the urban context, and the language used, represent a restored temple (21:16, 22–23). The Genesis concept of the earth as a planetary temple filled with God's image-bearers now finds fullness in Revelation. Unlike the Old Testament temple with its courts and veil that separated people from God, in the new creation,

---

10. In his judgement vision, John wrote that "if anyone's name was not found written in the book of life, he was thrown into the lake of fire" (20:15).

their relationship is unhindered by the effects of sin.[11] God's dwelling is with humanity (Rev 21:3).[12]

The place has unparalleled beauty. Sun and moon no longer exist, for God's glory provides continual light for the nations to walk in (Rev 21:23-24; cf. Isa 60:1-3, 11, 19-20). A river flows from the throne giving water to the tree of life that provides healing to the nations (Rev 22:2; cf. Ezek 47:12; Zech 14:8-9). Here is the permanent dwelling place of God and his people (Rev 21:3; Isa 25:8; Zech 13:9). John is intentional in describing the new heaven and earth with Eden-like qualities.[13] Life began in a garden; it will continue through eternity in a garden-like city. In the beginning, God's image-bearers had unrestrained access to him. What once was shall be again. This time, however, it will be even greater. God's image-bearers will fill the new earth, glorifying him and experiencing the fullness of joy and pleasures forevermore (Psalm 16:11). No wonder John ends his book with "Come Lord Jesus" (Rev 22:20)!

## CONCLUSION

Revelation not only concludes the New Testament, but takes readers back into the Old Testament. John draws deeply from Torah and the Prophets to provide a vision of what was and is to come. The difficult days foretold by Jesus in the Gospels comes to pass in Revelation. Churches were struggling to remain faithful to the mission of God. They needed hope, encouragement, and exhortation. They needed to see the bigger picture. John pulls back the curtain to reveal the sovereign over the world, Satan, and his church. He is faithful to his covenants, redeems and sustains his priests, and comes to judge evil and restore all things.

---

11.  David Mathewson, *A New Heaven and a New Earth: The Meaning and Function of the Old Testament in Revelation 21:1-22:5* (New York: Sheffield Academic, 2003), 114. For another perspective on the temple in Revelation see G. K. Beale, *The Temple and the Church's Mission*, 313-34.

12.  Mathewson, *A New Heaven and a New Earth*, 51.

13.  Mathewson writes "By alluding to Old Testament texts which portray the return of paradise conditions, John envisions the renewed Jerusalem as a source of perpetual life and well-being for its inhabitants (22.1-2)." *A New Heaven and a New Earth*, 220.

## REFLECTION QUESTIONS

1. What do you think John is attempting to accomplish by connecting so much of the Old Testament with Revelation?

2. What are your thoughts about the fact that many will die for the faith as part of God's mission in the world?

3. How does knowing that people from every nation, tribe, and language worship God in heaven affect the way the church should engage in mission today?

4. What are you doing to be intentionally involved in God's mission before he returns?

## CONCLUSION

# Reflections and Application to Contemporary Practice

THIS BOOK HAS covered a great deal of material in a brief space. This conclusion is an attempt to make a few points of application related to our study. While this list is not exhaustive, it is a starting point for continued thought, discussion, and adjustment.

### The church must give more attention to the Old Testament when it comes to understanding God's mission.

As new covenant believers, it is easy for the church to quickly return to the first century for understanding regarding her identity and purpose in the world. This is not a bad thing. The breakdown occurs whenever the church ignores the Old Testament. She forgets God. It is impossible for the church to understand both her identity in Christ and God's mission assigned to her apart from the Old Testament. For decades, the church was without the writings that came to be called the New Testament. While the apostolic teaching was present, so was the Old Testament. In fact, the apostolic teaching was grounded in the Old Testament.

God's mission did not begin in the first century; God's mission did not change in the first century. The church has an ancient heritage with deep roots. Contemporary preaching and teaching *must* connect the Great Commission to Torah, Prophets, and Writings. The Old Testament is relevant, especially when it comes to God's mission, for the modern believer.

## The church must bring biblical scholars, missiologists and missionaries together.

There is a long western tradition of dichotomizing biblical and theological studies from what used to be labeled "practical theology," a category that eventually included missions after missions became a department within the church's plethora of activities. While this has been a most unhealthy separation and categorization within the academy, the church has also suffered deeply. Biblical scholars must move beyond theory and study divorced from field-based realities. Missiologists and missionaries must move beyond field-based realities divorced from Scripture. These parties deeply need each other. Paul had much to say to the Corinthians about how the body suffers when one part suffers. Sometimes these parties look askance toward one another. One party views the other as atheological, prooftexting methods and strategy, and more concerned with telling stories grounded in social studies. The other party is troubled when men and women pour hours of time into examination and discussion of a Greek or Hebrew word and never make any connection to gospel advancement among the five billion people who are lost without Christ. Brothers and sisters, we are not in competition with one another. Rather, we are collaborators in the mission of God.

## The church must continue to develop the theological foundation for global disciple making on more than just a few isolated New Testament verses.

This is clearly related to the aforementioned need of the body of Christ to work together. Our missiology must rest upon the foundation of an exegetical theology. While there is great value in drawing from the social sciences, managerial and leadership studies, business, linguistics, communication studies, and others, the church has often embraced these disciplines to an unhealthy degree. Yes, all truth is God's truth wherever it may be found. But, not all of God's truth should be applied to the church. A biblical theology of mission will help alleviate the unhealthy appropriation and application of God's truths in the improper spheres.

This requires moving well beyond a few passages for the church's actions in the world. There is a robust theological framework found in Genesis-Revelation. This framework establishes wide and healthy parameters in which our methods and strategies can exist. It is not a narrow set of boundaries. It is divinely designed to exist in any cultural context, at any time, among any people.

### The church must revisit the apostolic nature of her sent-ness into the world and consider what should be her priorities.

Even after all of the *missio Dei* discussions of the last eighty years, mission lacks clarity of definition. When God's mission is nebulous, the actions (i.e., missions) of the church become multifaceted and even contradictory. We have arrived at a time when everything the church does is missions, even if the gospel is never shared. The following question needs to be addressed: "What is the apostolic nature and function of the church?" If God is an apostolic God, then the manifestation of his mission in the world will have practical implications on the actions of his people in the world. This includes coming to a greater understanding and application of what Jesus modeled and what was reproduced in his disciples and church. Of course, there are aspects of the Messiah exclusive to his life and work. But, the apostolic priorities and functions described in the first century, did not start with the Jerusalem Church. There has always been a prioritization of actions and goals to be accomplished throughout the Old and New Testaments. God the Father gave distinction to certain matters in carrying out his mission. God the Son and God the Spirit did likewise. The apostles and first century church also gave priority to their actions based on what God revealed.

# Bibliography

Anderson, A. A. *Psalms (73-150)*. The New Century Bible Commentary. Grand Rapids: Eerdmans, 1972.

Ashcraft, Morris. *Revelation*. Vol. 12 of *The Broadman Bible Commentary*. Nashville: Broadman & Holman, 1972.

Baldwin, Joyce G. *Haggai, Zechariah and Malachi: An Introduction and Commentary*. Downers Grove, IL: InterVarsity Press, 1972.

Barth, Karl. "An Exegetical Study of Matthew 28:16-20." In *The Theology of the Christian Mission*, edited by Gerald H. Anderson, 55-71. Nashville: Abingdon, 1961.

Bauckham, Richard. *Bible and Mission: Christian Witness in a Postmodern World*. Grand Rapids: Baker Books, 2003.

———. *The Climax of Prophecy: Studies on the Book of Revelation*. Edinburgh: T&T Clark, 1993.

Beal, G. K. *A New Testament Biblical Theology: The Unfolding of the Old Testament in the New*. Grand Rapids: Baker Academic, 2011.

———. *The Temple and the Church's Mission: A Biblical Theology of the Dwelling Place of God*. Downers Grove, IL: InterVarsity Press, 2004.

Beeby, Harry Daniel. "A Missional Approach to Renewed Interpretation." In *Renewing Biblical Interpretation*, edited by Craig Bartholomew, Colin Greene, and Karl Möller, 268-83. Grand Rapids: Zondervan, 2000.

———. *Canon and Mission*. Harrisburg, PA: Trinity Press International, 1999.

Bird, Michael F. *Jesus and the Origins of the Gentile Mission*. New York: T&T Clark, 2007.

Blackburn, W. Ross. *The God Who Makes Himself Known: The Missionary Heart of the Book of Exodus*. Downers Grove, IL: InterVarsity Press, 2012.

Blauw, Johannes. *The Missionary Nature of the Church: A Survey of the Biblical Theology of Mission.* New York: McGraw-Hill, 1962.

Blomberg, Craig. *Matthew.* Nashville: Broadman & Holman, 1992.

Bock, Darrell L. "The Use of the Old Testament in Luke-Acts: Christology and Mission." Pages 494–511 in *Society of Biblical Literature 1990 Seminary Papers.* SBLSPS 29. Atlanta: Society of Biblical Literature, 1990.

Boda, Mark J. "Declare his Glory Among the Nations." In *Christian Mission: Old Testament Foundations and New Testament Developments,* edited by Stanley E. Porter and Cynthia Long Westfall, 13–41. Eugene, OR: Pickwick, 2011.

Bosch, David J. "Hermeneutical Principles in the Biblical Foundation for Mission." *Evangelical Review of Theology* 17 (1993): 437–51.

——. *Transforming Mission: Paradigm Shifts in Theology of Mission.* Maryknoll, NY: Orbis Books, 1991.

Bowers, Paul. "Church and Mission in Paul." *Journal for the Study of the New Testament* 44 (1991): 89–111.

Bruce, F. F. *The Gospel of John: Introduction, Exposition, and Notes.* Grand Rapids: Eerdmans, 1983.

——. *Paul: Apostle of the Heart Set Free.* Grand Rapids: Eerdmans, 1977.

Caird, G. B. *A Commentary on the Revelation of St. John the Divine.* New York: Harper & Row, 1966.

Carson, D. A. *The Gospel According to John.* Grand Rapids: Eerdmans, 1991.

Chin, Moses. "A Heavenly Home for the Homeless." *Tyndale Bulletin* 42, no. 1 (May 1991): 96–112.

Cole, R. Alan. *Mark: An Introduction and Commentary.* Grand Rapids: Eerdmans, 1961.

DuBose, Francis M. *God Who Sends: A Fresh Quest for Biblical Mission.* Nashville: Broadman & Holman, 1983.

Dumbrell, William J. "Abraham and the Abrahamic Covenant in Galatians 3:1–14." In *The Gospel to the Nations: Perspectives on Paul's Mission,* edited by Peter Bolt and Mark Thompson, 19–31. Downers Grove, IL: InterVarsity Press, 2000.

Elwell, Walter A. and Robert W. Yarbrough. *Encountering the New Testament: A Historical and Theological Survey.* 3rd ed. Grand Rapids: Baker Academic, 2013.

Fee, Gordon D. and Douglas Stuart. *How to Read the Bible for All Its Worth: A Guide to Understanding the Bible.* Grand Rapids: Zondervan, 1981.

Filbeck, David. *Yes, God of the Gentiles, Too: The Missionary Message of the Old Testament.* Wheaton, IL: Billy Graham Center, 1994.

Flemming, Dean. *Recovering the Full Mission of God: A Biblical Perspective on Being, Doing and Telling.* Downers Grove, IL: IVP Academic, 2013.

Garrett, Duane A. *Hosea, Joel.* Nashville: Broadman and Holman, 1997.

Gentry, Peter J. and Stephen J. Wellum. *Kingdom through Covenant: A Biblical-Theological Understanding of the Covenants.* 2nd ed. Wheaton, IL: Crossway, 2018.

———. *Kingdom through Covenant: A Biblical-Theological Understanding of the Covenants.* Wheaton, IL: Crossway, 2012.

Gilliland, Dean S. *Pauline Theology and Mission Practice.* Grand Rapids: Baker Books, 1983.

Glasser, Arthur F. *Announcing the Kingdom: The Story of God's Mission in the Bible.* Grand Rapids: Baker Academic, 2003.

Goerner, Henry Cornell. *Thus It is Written: The Missionary Motif in the Scriptures.* Nashville: Broadman & Holman, 1944.

Goheen, Michael W. *A Light to the Nations: The Missional Church and the Biblical Story.* Grand Rapids: Baker Academic, 2011.

Goldingay, John. *Theological Diversity and the Authority of the Old Testament.* Grand Rapids: Eerdmans, 1987.

Goldsworthy, Graeme. "Biblical Theology and the Shape of Paul's Mission." In *The Gospel to the Nations: Perspectives on Paul's Mission,* edited by Peter Bolt and Mark Thompson. Downers Grove, IL: InterVarsity Press, 2000.

———. *The Gospel in Revelation: Gospel and Apocalypse.* Milton Keynes, UK: Paternoster, 1984.

Gorman, Michael J. *Reading Revelation Responsibly: Uncivil Worship and Witness: Following the Lamb into the New Creation.* Eugene, OR: Cascade Books, 2011.

Hahn, Ferdinand. *Mission in the New Testament.* Naperville, IL: Alec R. Allenson, 1965.

Harvey, John D. "Mission in Jesus' Teaching." In *Mission in the New Testament: An Evangelical Approach,* edited by William J. Larkin Jr. and Joel F. Williams, 30–49. Maryknoll, NY: Orbis Books, 1998.

Harris, R. Geoffrey. *Mission in the Gospels*. n.p.: Epworth, 2004.

Hengel, Martin. *Between Jesus and Paul: Studies in the Earliest History of Christianity*. Philadelphia: Fortress, 1983.

Hiebert, Paul G. "Evangelism, Church, and Kingdom." In *The Good News of the Kingdom: Mission Theology for the Third Millennium*, edited by Charles Van Engen, Dean S. Gilliland, and Paul Pierson, 153-61. Maryknoll, NY: Orbis Books, 1993.

Hill, Andrew E., and John H. Walton. *A Survey of the Old Testament*. Grand Rapids: Zondervan, 1991.

Hogg, William Richey. "Psalm 22 and Christian Mission: A Reflection." *International Review of Mission* 77, no. 306 (April 1988): 238-46.

House, Paul R., and Eric Mitchell. *Old Testament Survey*. 2nd ed. Nashville: B&H Academic, 2007.

Howell, Jr., Don N. "Mission in Paul's Epistles: Theological Bearings." In *Mission in the New Testament: An Evangelical Approach*, edited by William J. Larkin, Jr. and Joel F. Williams, 92-116. Maryknoll, NY: Orbis Books, 1998.

Huey, F. B. *Jeremiah, Lamentations*. Nashville: Broadman & Holman, 1993.

Hultgren, Arland J. "Paul's Christology and His Mission to the Gentiles." In *Paul as Missionary: Identity, Activity, Theology, and Practice*, edited by Trevor J. Burke and Brian S. Rosener, 115-27. New York: T&T Clark, 2011.

Hunsberger, George R. "Proposals for a Missional Hermeneutic: Mapping a Conversation." *Missiology* 39, no. 3 (July 2011): 309-21.

Jeremias, Joachim. *Jesus' Promise to the Nations*. Translated by S. H. Hooke. Naperville, IL: Alec R. Allenson, 1958.

Kaiser, Jr., Walter C. *Mission in the Old Testament: Israel as a Light to the Nations*. 2nd ed. Grand Rapids: Baker Academic, 2012.

Keener, Craig S. "Sent Like Jesus: Johannine Missiology (John 20:21-22)." *Asian Journal of Pentecostal Studies* 12, no. 1 (2009): 21-45.

Kidner, Derek. *Psalms 73-150*. Downers Grove, IL: IVP Academic, 1975.

———. *Psalms 1-72*. Downers Grove, IL: IVP Academic, 1973.

———. *Genesis: An Introduction and Commentary*. Downers Grove, IL: InterVarsity Press, 1967.

Köstenberger, Andreas J. "Mission in the General Epistles." In *Mission in the New Testament: An Evangelical Approach*, edited by William

J. Larkin, Jr., and Joel F. Williams, 189–206. Maryknoll, NY: Orbis Books, 1998.

———. *The Missions of Jesus and the Disciples According to the Fourth Gospel.* Grand Rapids: Eerdmans, 1998.

Köstenberger, Andreas J. and Peter T. O'Brien. *Salvation to the Ends of the Earth: A Biblical Theology of Mission.* Downers Grove, IL: InterVarsity Press, 2001.

Landon, Michael. "The Psalms as Mission." *Restoration Quarterly* 44, no. 3 (2002): 165–75.

Legrand, Lucien. *Unity and Plurality: Mission in the Bible.* Translated by Robert R. Barr. Maryknoll, NY: Orbis Books, 1990.

Longman III, Tremper. *Psalms: An Introduction and Commentary.* Downers Grove, IL: InterVarsity Press, 2014.

Magda, Ksenija. *Paul's Territoriality and Mission Strategy.* Tübingen: Mohr Siebeck, 2009.

Maré, Leonard P. "Israel's Praise as Enactment of the Gospel: Psalm 96 in Missiological Context." *Missionalia* 34, no. 2/3 (Aug–Nov 2006): 395–407.

Marlowe, W. Creighton. "Music of Missions: Themes of Cross-Cultural Outreach in the Psalms." *Missiology* 26, no. 4 (October 1998): 445–56.

Martin-Achard, Robert. *A Light to the Nations: A Study of the Old Testament Conception of Israel's Mission to the World.* Edinburgh: Oliver & Boyd, 1962.

Marshall, I. Howard. *The Acts of the Apostles: An Introduction and Commentary.* Grand Rapids: Eerdmans, 1980.

Matthews, Kenneth A. *Genesis 11:27–50:26.* Nashville: Broadman & Holman, 2005.

Matthewson, David. *A New Heaven and a New Earth: The Meaning and Function of the Old Testament in Revelation 21:1–22:5.* New York: Sheffield Academic, 2003.

McIntosh, John A. "Missio Dei." In *Evangelical Dictionary of World Missions,* edited by A. Scott Moreau, 631–33. Grand Rapids: Baker Books, 2000.

McNicol, Allan J. *The Conversion of the Nations in Revelation.* New York: T&T Clark, 2011.

McPolin, James. "Mission in the Fourth Gospel." *The Irish Theological Quarterly* 36, no. 2 (April 1969): 113–22.

McQuilkin, J. Robertson. "An Evangelical Assessment of Mission Theology of the Kingdom of God." In *The Good News of the Kingdom: Mission Theology for the Third Millennium*, edited by Charles Van Engen, Dean S. Gilliland, and Paul Pierson, 172–78. Maryknoll, NY: Orbis Books, 1993.

Meek, James A. *The Gentile Mission in Old Testament Citations in Acts: Text, Hermeneutic, and Purpose.* London: T&T Clark, 2008.

Middleton, J. Richard. *A New Heaven and a New Earth: Reclaiming Biblical Eschatology.* Grand Rapids: Baker Academic, 2014.

Miller, Robert D. "The Gentiles in the Zion Hymns: Canaanite Myth and Christian Mission." *Transformation* 26, no. 4 (October 2009): 232–46.

Morris, Leon. *The Epistle to the Romans.* Grand Rapids: Eerdmans, 1988.

Motyer, J. Alec. *Isaiah: An Introduction and Commentary.* Downers Grove, IL: InterVarsity Press, 1999.

Newbigin, Lesslie. *The Open Secret: An Introduction to the Theology of Mission.* Rev. ed. Grand Rapids: Eerdmans, 1995.

Nissen, Johannes. *New Testament and Missions: Historical and Hermeneutical Perspectives.* 3rd ed. Frankfurt: Peter Lang, 2004.

O'Brien, P. T. *Gospel and Mission in the Writings of Paul: An Exegetical and Theological Analysis.* Grand Rapids: Baker Books, 1993.

O'Connor, Dan. "Holiness of Life as a Way of Christian Witness." *International Review of Mission* 80, no. 317 (Jan 1991): 17–26.

Okoye, James Chukwuma. *Israel and the Nations: A Mission Theology of the Old Testament.* Maryknoll, NY: Orbis Books, 2006.

Okure, Teresa. *The Johannine Approach to Mission: A Contextual Study of John 4:1–42.* Tübingen: J. C. B. Mohr (Paul Siebeck), 1988.

Ott, Craig, Stephen J. Strauss, and Timothy C. Tennent. *Encountering Theology of Mission: Biblical Foundations, Historical Developments, and Contemporary Issues.* Grand Rapids: Baker Academic, 2010.

Payne, J. D. *Apostolic Church Planting: Birthing New Churches from New Believers.* Downers Grove, IL: InterVaristy Press, 2015.

———. *Discovering Church Planting: An Introduction to the Whats, Whys, and Hows of Global Church Planting.* Downers Grove, IL: InterVarsity Press, 2009.

Peters, George W. *A Biblical Theology of Missions*. Chicago: Moody Press, 1972.

Plummer, Robert L. *Paul's Understanding of the Church's Mission: Did the Apostle Paul Expect the Early Christian Communities to Evangelize?*. Eugene, OR: Wipf & Stock, 2006.

Polhill, John B. *Acts*. Nashville: Broadman & Holman, 1992.

Robinson, P. J. "Some Missiological Perspectives from 1 Peter 2:4-10." *Missionalia* 17, no. 3 (November 1989): 176-87.

Rowley, H. H. *The Missionary Message of the Old Testament*. London: The Carey Kingsgate Press, 1944.

Schnabel, Eckhard J. *Early Christian Mission: Jesus and the Twelve*. Vol. 1 of *Early Christian Mission*. Downers Grove, IL: InterVarsity Press, 2004.

——. *Early Christian Mission: Paul and the Early Church*. Vol. 2 of *Early Christian Mission*. Downers Grove, IL: InterVarsity Press, 2004.

——. "John and the Future of the Nations." *Bulletin for Biblical Research* 12, no. 2 (2002): 243-71.

Scobie, Charles H. H. *The Ways of Our God: An Approach to Biblical Theology*. Grand Rapids: Eerdmans, 2003.

——. "Israel and the Nations: An Essay in Biblical Theology." *Tyndale Bulletin* 43, no. 2 (1992): 283-305.

Scott, James M. *Paul and the Nations: The Old Testament and Jewish Background of Paul's Mission to the Nations with Special Reference to the Destination of Galatians*. Tübingen: J. C B. Mohr (Paul Siebeck), 1995.

Senior, Donald and Carroll Stuhlmueller. *The Biblical Foundations for Mission*. Maryknoll, NY: Orbis Books, 1983.

Spitters, Denny and Matthew Ellison. *When Everything is Missions*. n.p.: Bottom Line Media, 2017.

Stein, Robert H. *Luke*. Nashville: Broadman & Holman, 1992.

Steuernagel, Vladir R. "An Exiled Community as a Missionary Community: A Study Based on 1 Peter 2:9, 10." *Evangelical Review of Theology* 40, no. 3 (2016): 196-204.

Sundkler, Bengt. "Jésus et les Païens." *Revue d'histoire et de Philosophie Religieuses* (Novembre-Décembre 1936): 462-99.

Taber, Charles R. "Missiology and the Bible." *Missiology* 11, no. 2 (April 1983): 229-45.

Walls, Andrew F. "Mission History as the Substructure of Mission
   Theology." *Swedish Missiological Themes* 93, no. 3 (2005): 367–78.

Ware, James P. *Paul and the Mission of the Church: Philippians in Ancient
   Jewish Context.* Grand Rapids: Baker Academic, 2011.

Wenham, Gordon J. *Genesis 1–15.* Dallas: Word, 1998.

Wilson, Stephen G. *Gentiles and the Gentile Mission in Luke–Acts.*
   Cambridge: Cambridge University Press, 1973.

Wright, Christopher J. H. *The Mission of God: Unlocking the Bible's Grand
   Narrative.* Downers Grove, IL: IVP Academic, 2006.

———. "Mission as a Matrix for Hermeneutics and Biblical Theology." In
   *Out of Egypt: Biblical Theology and Biblical Interpretation,* edited by
   Craig Bartholomew, Mary Healy, and Karl Möller, 102–43. Grand
   Rapids: Zondervan, 2004.

———. "Old Testament Theology of Mission." In *Evangelical Dictionary of
   World Missions,* edited by A. Scott Moreau, 706–09. Grand Rapids:
   Baker Books, 2000.

———. *Deuteronomy.* Peabody, MA: Hendrickson, 1996.

Wright, N. T. "The Bible and Christian Mission." In *Scripture and Its
   Interpretation: A Global, Ecumenical Introduction to the Bible,* edited
   by Michael J. Gorman, 388–400. Grand Rapids: Baker Academic,
   2017.

Vicedom, Georg F. *The Mission of God: An Introduction to a Theology of
   Mission.* St. Louis: Concordia, 1965.

# Subject Index

# Scripture Index

## OLD TESTAMENT

Christian Mission

A CONCISE
GLOBAL HISTORY

———

EDWARD L. SMITHER

# ALSO AVAILABLE
# FROM LEXHAM PRESS

*Christian Mission: A Concise Global History*

———

**Visit lexhampress.com to learn more**